THE UNASHAMED GUIDE TO

Virtual Management   🔍

Virtual Workforce

Virtual Teams

Virtual Meetings

Virtual Office Romances

Ben Bisbee and Kathy Wisniewski

ATD Press is an internationally renowned source of insightful and practical information on talent development, training, and professional development.

ATD Press
1640 King Street
Alexandria, VA 22314 USA

Ordering information: Books published by ATD Press can be purchased by visiting ATD's website at www.td.org/books or by calling 800.628.2783 or 703.683.8100.

Library of Congress Control Number: 2019945544

ISBN-10: 1-949036-55-3
ISBN-13: 978-1-949036-55-8
e-ISBN: 978-1-949036-56-5

ATD Press Editorial Staff
Director: Sarah Halgas
Manager: Melissa Jones
Community of Practice Manager, Management: Ryan Changcoco
Developmental Editor: Jack Harlow
Text Design: Shirley E.M. Raybuck
Cover Design: Lindy Martin, Faceout Studio

Printed by Versa Press, East Peoria, IL

Contents

Culture Is King:
Understanding and Building Virtual Teams 129

Home vs. Home Office:
Addressing Procedure With (or Without) a Policy 177

Introduction

It had come to this again: We had to turn to Google. A friend who was a manager for a virtual workplace contacted us to ask if we knew how to deal with an online office romance that had recently bloomed. They needed to know the best way to handle the situation and couldn't find anything relatable or tailored to the virtual workplace. They came to us because they assumed we'd know a few things. We do—but this was new to us.

So we did some online searching, but came away empty-handed. There were no answers. Sure, we found a ton of stuff about general stationary office romance issues and a few articles related to the merits and wonder of loving virtual employment. But nothing that really helped this specific situation that needed its own level of detail and nuance for the virtual world.

It was at this point we realized something distressing: We, and countless other virtual managers, were completely on our own. We also saw an opportunity.

That moment sparked the very idea for this book. What if we didn't have to blindly search the Internet for solutions to our virtual workplace problems, hoping for a link that would lead to some shred of an answer? What if we didn't have to awkwardly tap our friends on the shoulder to ask for their advice or insights every time we tried to make sense of managing employees in a virtual world? What if there was a guide that gave us all the answers, or at least offered a range of suggestions?

We're Far Past the Early Stages

The problem as we see it is that most current conversations, articles, books, or blogs related to virtual employment are still very much driven by the building-block arguments for establishing or attempting virtual employment. That is, they're still deeply rooted in "why" and "when" when most of us who have been in this space—some for well over a decade—are anxiously focused on the "how" of our needs.

We believe new and established professionals working in virtual environments no longer need convincing of the possibility or plausibility of virtual employment. Those formative days have passed. In fact, 4.3 million employees now work from home at least half the time. Virtual or work-at-home employment, among the non-self-employed population, has grown by 140 percent since 2005, nearly 10 times faster than the rest of the workforce or the self-employed (Global Workplace Analytics 2018). These professionals are seeking real virtual solutions to their daily virtual issues.

And like humans themselves, the solutions necessary for a wide variety of issues are never one-size-fits-all. However, when solutions are presented, we need stronger ideas, tools, and guidance to leverage them as actual policies and practices. We're essentially past "suggestions" as just suggestions. We need suggestions that come with instructions and intended outcomes.

So beyond taking the conversation on its natural progression in the virtual industry, this book also includes the advice of real professionals and experts who work virtually across a wealth of sectors. Within these pages they share and unpack virtual workplace realities beyond your wildest expectations, covering tales and topics that may have once been considered untouchable or implausible in a virtual setting. Are we going to address virtual workplace romance? Absolutely. But we're also going to be talking about such topics as identifying online cliques, secret Santa, virtual disciplinary action, taking meetings on the toilet, and so much more.

Get ready; when we say this is the "unashamed guide" we are not kidding around. But there is a method to our madness! Within this book we have built a model to help you think beyond "answers" to questions, so you can discover the necessary building blocks for solutions to problems.

Who You Are Matters

So who are you anyway, reader? In our minds, you are a smart and savvy manager working virtually yourself or managing at least one virtual employee. You have all the technology you need and you crave tactics for management that are similar—extraordinarily similar—to managers in stationary workplaces, but the situation is just different enough that you need a few extra pointers, skills, or insights.

This book is packed with information that will aid just about anyone in any setting—even volunteers—who find themselves facing virtual management problems in a modern world. But for the purpose of this book, we are going to talk to you as a classic middle manager. Why? Because we believe middle managers make the world go round—they are the everyday heroes of any organization, making the magic happen, with their fingers on the pulse of the day-to-day dealings in the working world.

We also believe that middle management is one of the best advocates of day-to-day needs at any organization. They have to deal with issues in real time and are often the first ones searching frantically for some shred of policy or purpose-driven tool to aid them in a tricky situation. So cheers to you, our middle management friends! This book has your needs in mind and will often speak to the very heart of your wants, desires, and plights.

The 4Ps of Virtual Solutions

As we mentioned, we have real solutions for real problems. And like the very technology we use every day, the building blocks of virtual solutions for our everyday problems are layered and complicated. Our job as authors is to make it feel as thoughtful, easy, and effortless as possible. We're doing this by presenting what we call the 4Ps of Virtual Solutions. These 4Ps represent the four critical areas you need to access and address to turn suggestions into workplace practice and policy:

- **Purpose.** What is the reason you're doing or addressing something? Simply put, begin with "why." Why is this an issue? What does this need to be solved? Why does this matter in your virtual workplace?

- **Personality.** How is the topic at hand best addressed at the human level, by your employees, as organizational culture? How does this topic relate to your organization? And how does your approach to these processes and policies reflect the personality of your organization?

- **Policy.** What are the rules or principles associated with the topics at hand? How are they expressed and how does an employee learn about or access them?

- **Process.** What are the series of actions or steps taken to achieve a particular end related to this topic? How does tech play a role? How will you address solutions to problems as a company? How do the policies you set forth become everyday solutions or problem solvers?

At the end of the day, the 4Ps are also just really good feedback loop topic areas that will help you look at any problem you have virtually with a new set of eyes aimed at solving them.

Now a fair warning is needed. This book isn't about creating a one-size-fits-all virtual reality. Rather, it provides a wealth of perspectives from diverse angles—sometimes the answer you're seeking has *five* different variables. For example, there may be five different versions of technology, and while some may be better than others, there might also be essentially no major difference and it's more about your approach. Or those variables could be associated with money, creativity, or sensitivity. And sometimes it doesn't matter, because you just need a quick fix. In any case, you'll find this book offers options to ensure that no matter the solution or your problem, you'll be able to evaluate its purpose, determine how it fits within your organizational personality, and then implement a process to help make it stick.

Unashamed Is the Name of the Game

Are you ready? We're excited for you to come along with us on this journey to navigate the intricacies of the world of virtual employment, which are similar to, but also often extremely different from, those associated with traditional stationary workplace settings.

Our goal is for you to use this book as a guide—something to return to time after time to find tips and guidance for whatever area of virtual management you are seeking to improve, unpack, or solve. As such, we've broken things down into hyper-specific topic-based chapters—30 of them, in fact. But to make this guidebook useful, we've grouped these topics into four over-arching sections:

- **Game of Zones.** This section sets the stage and covers topics truly unique to the virtual workplace, such as time zones, working hours, flexible schedules, and privacy.
- **The New VHR.** This section covers the core aspects of managing, but with a virtual spin. Topics include hiring and interviews, onboarding, meetings, performance reviews, and firings.
- **Culture Is King.** This section focuses on how you build and maintain a virtual team. Just because you're virtual doesn't mean you can neglect the importance that team building and culture can play in a workplace. You need to keep an eye on employee morale, cliques, and gossip, while also bringing the team together with virtual parties and benefits.
- **Home vs. Home Office.** This section offers advice on handling the daily oddities of working from home. Whether it's laundry, errands, meetings from the bathroom, office romance, or interruptive pets and children, you should be aware of how to address these topics.

From the mundane to the awkward, we are going to cover it all, because we know you have to manage it all no matter where you are managing from. May you enjoy this journey of solution-ing your problems as much as we enjoyed writing solutions for your problems.

Have a suggestion or story related to any topic covered in this book? Share it online at www.unashamedvirtualmanagement .com and it might be featured on the book's website and in future editions!

GAME OF ZONES

Understanding the Virtual World

1.

All About Time Zones

It's the subject of songs, books, poems, movies, and religious texts. A most precious commodity. We never have enough of it, yet sometimes we have too much of it on our hands. Occasionally we borrow it, sometimes it flies, and at other times it just stands still. Sometimes we waste it, and at other moments it's on our side. We try desperately to manage it but often feel that it really manages us. What is it? Time.

Such mighty juxtaposition for such a tiny little word. We all have the same 24 hours to work with. We are all very busy. And now, thanks to technology, we have the easiest access we have ever had to people on the other side of the globe.

Let's Level Set, Shall We?

You may have never thought about it this way, but working with another person in another part of the world creates a virtual workplace. Even if the rest of your co-workers are surrounding you in cubicleland, that single co-worker in different time zone or country makes you a member of the virtual workplace club!

Welcome. And while working with those in other time zones has its advantages, it also has its challenges.

The biggest is most definitely time differences. You have to search and calculate the exact time difference between where you are and the country on the other end. You work forward—and backward and forward again—and then when you finally schedule your meeting, you realize you didn't take Europe's daylight saving time into account (which, in case you didn't know, is different than the United States's) and someone ends up missing the meeting.

So here you are, playing a very tricky, very sophisticated game of zones. But what are the most important things to keep in mind when strategizing your next move? Let's get started.

Manage Your Own Expectations

When working with people from around the globe, the most important piece of advice we can offer is to manage your own expectations. In this highly technological age, we have become accustomed to receiving immediate or semi-immediate responses when reaching out for information. We send an email, we get a response shortly thereafter. We expect it, like a dog gets used to getting a treat every time he performs a trick or command. But what happens when that dog doesn't get his treat immediately? He gets impatient, annoyed, agitated until he gets what he wants or, more significantly, what he has come to expect. In the United States, it's often difficult for us to wait for a response when we're on the East Coast and we've sent an email to someone on the West Coast, which is a mere three hours behind. U.S. time differences can be even greater—there are four hours between the East Coast and Alaska and five or six hours between the East Coast and

Hawaii (which does *not* participate in daylight saving time). When you take a typical nine to five workday into consideration, six hours is a *lot*!

But consider what it's like if you're on the East Coast and you send an email to someone in, say, South Korea, which is 13 hours ahead. Let's say you sent that email around noon your time. What time did it hit the inbox of the person in Korea? (You didn't think we were going to make you do math in this book, did ya?) You guessed it! They received it at 1 a.m., when they're more likely to be sleeping than online checking email. And by the time they *do* see your email, *you'll* be the one who's asleep! And furthermore, how often do we wait to respond to emails because we have to gather information, talk to someone higher up, jet off to a meeting, or take care of something else that simply takes higher priority at the moment?

The game of zones becomes a waiting game, and a response may take significantly longer to receive. However, the opportunity to collaborate with and leverage the vast global talent pool far outweighs the small challenges it presents. So, manage your own expectations. Think ahead and be patient!

Blessed Are the Flexible, For They Will Not Break

Take a scenario like the one presented above. Now, remove "email" and insert "conference call."

Now stop groaning.

Flexibility is the name of the game when it comes to working with global teams and global time zones. When you have to consider time zones that are a full 12 hours (or more) apart, you *must* time conference calls very carefully to accommodate everyone. This requires flexibility and a whole new level of commitment from you and your team.

> *One virtual position that I held required me to plan the annual meeting for a professional membership group. In 2017 their meeting was held in Singapore, a full 12-hour difference from where I was located.*
>
> *When sending emails to my contacts there, I had to think ahead about the information I was seeking. I learned to not expect an answer until the next working day because when I was sending the email, they were either not working or fast asleep. We also had to set up phone calls several times throughout the process to discuss details. We decided to switch times every call—one would be 9 a.m. my time and 9 p.m. theirs, and the next time, we would flip. This required flexibility on both our parts, but it worked out perfectly in the end.*
>
> —Kathy

One tip is to consider flipping conference calls each time when your team members are this spread out. This means that sacrificing some of your own "off hours" to make the 12-hour time difference conference call work. For example, if your monthly call happens at 9 a.m. your time (which equals 9 p.m. their time), consider swapping the time for the next call. This helps create a more fair environment, because everyone equally sacrifices their personal time. You don't want anyone feeling like they're not cared about or considered, or resentment may start to build.

This might be a new concept for you. Sometimes when people work a strict nine-to-five job, they believe that their off time is their time off. Fair enough. It may be challenging to adopt a new way of working or thinking. We get it. But working globally means thinking globally. And we would say again that the benefits of remote work and the ability to interact and work closely with people all over the globe is exciting and beneficial and will yield very positive influences on your company or organization. So, be flexible. Flexible people bend—they don't break. Embrace the vast and diverse possibilities! You'll be glad you did!

Culture

When working with people around the globe, you will experience many cultural differences. Did you know that in Singapore, for example, if a bus company says they're picking you up at midnight, you had *better* be there at midnight? In an experience that Kathy had, when she asked the bus company why they didn't wait for her party, their answer was "We did wait. The driver left at 12:01!"

You need to do a little research. Much like the Myers-Briggs personality test can give you great insight into how other people tick, a little research on the culture of the country you're working with can go a long way in helping avoid unnecessary faux pas and embarrassment. You can find all sorts of information about this online. Or better yet? Ask the person you're working with! Who is going to turn you down the opportunity to answer questions about their culture? Plus, this kind of research—talking with the person you're working with—will provide much more relevant cultural information. And as a bonus? You'll build a nice rapport with that person, who will appreciate that you took an interest in them and their culture.

Language and expressions are other important cultural considerations. Once, Ben was working with a global committee at the United Nations when he got on a conference call with 15 people who represented just about every major continent. While English was the working language, it didn't mean everyone knew everyone else's colloquialisms or turns of phrase. So, when Ben made the mistake of saying "Now this topic might take us down a very strange rabbit hole," he meant to imply that it would bring up a variety of additional topics that he didn't want to explore. Instead it brought about an unnecessary 20-minute conversation about what a "rabbit hole" had to do with the topic, and why we didn't want to travel down one. We would say in this instance, it's important to think not just about the game of zones, but the game of causal language too. Our advice here is to keep it simple. When working with people from other cultures and countries, the simpler the language, the better.

National culture is a consideration that you should not take lightly. A person's culture is a part of their very being, so taking the time to learn about someone and the values and norms that they have woven into their identity will level-up your working relationships and minimize the risk of offending a valuable team member.

Cultural differences are no less visible in a virtual workspace than in an in-person environment. I remember a U.S.-based project manager insisting that she didn't have to deal with cultural differences on her global team because everyone lived and worked in their countries of origin. Almost that moment her phone rang, and she excused herself—it was her colleague in India. When she returned from the call, she spent a long time lamenting how her colleagues India and China didn't understand work-life balance, expecting her to be available to them 24/7.

—Caliopy Glaros, Founder and Principal Consultant,
Philanthropy Without Borders

A Few More Thoughts

That's our take on how to best handle the game of zones. You may also have organizational policies outlining how to deal with these situations, but we hope these help to fill any holes. You may think you've got it handled, but we'd just be up sick all night if we didn't at least mention them one more time:

✓ **Manage your expectations.**

✓ **Use technology wisely.** Take advantage of smart tools to help when working with people in various time zones.

✓ **Be flexible and understanding, but also try to be consistent.** That way everyone on the team can anticipate things like emails, deliverables, and expectations.

✓ **Do your research on culture.** Build a great rapport with your international co-workers by asking about their culture and what is important to them as part of the virtual workplace growth. You should also make sure everyone is working with the same tools and expectations.

✓ **Be proactive.** Think through conference call schedules and be mindful of time differences. Plan ahead so you can send emails (especially those of a somewhat urgent nature) well in advance to allow for the time difference and include ample time to await a response.

✓ **Be inclusive.** If you really want to show your international colleagues that you appreciate their culture, learn and use simple phrases in their language such as "hello," "goodbye," "please," and "thank you."

Signing Off

It is an exciting time. We have the privilege of interacting with and getting to know people from all around the globe, something that just two or three decades ago was practically impossible without actual, physical travel. This paved the way for the virtual workplace to exist. Proving we could work virtually and successfully with individuals around the world meant we could and should consider doing the same with those just one or more time zones away. Don't ever forget that. We are wise to take this privilege and leverage it for our mutual greatest success as opposed to assuming that something as minor as time differences could derail the whole process. Look to the opportunities that our global community presents and prepare for them wisely! When we can make a 12-hour time difference work, we are capable of just about anything in the virtual workplace, and that's something worth celebrating no matter where you are, no matter when you are.

2.

What Is Nine-to-Five in a Global, Virtual Workplace?

Being able to work in a global workplace has its advantages. You can leverage the knowledge and experience of those located all around the world, rather than be limited to those in your immediate geographic area. But while the benefits are great, this also comes with challenges and considerations—namely, what does nine-to-five look like in a global workplace?

Let's Level Set, Shall We?

You've probably heard the saying "It's five o'clock somewhere!" (often used in reference to the appropriate time to start drinking). Or maybe you've watched New Year's Eve celebrations on TV when they jump to midnight coverage of different cities around the world—but you still have several hours to go until your official "new year" begins. These are obvious examples of how we don't all follow the same clock.

Maybe your business has remote employees who are all in the same geographic area, or at least the same time zone. If that's the case, this chapter is not for you. However, if you are working with remote employees who are on a clock that differs even one hour from yours, you may have wondered what a nine-to-five schedule looks like for your team and company. It's an important question.

If, for example, your working hours are literally 9 a.m. to 5 p.m., what sort of expectations need to be set with someone on the other side of the world? Is the work time overlap of just one to three hours sufficient for getting work done efficiently or effectively for a team with one person working in Eastern Time, one person working in Europe (five to seven hours ahead), and a third person working in Singapore (a 12-hour difference)?

The Short Answer

The short answer is it's up to you or your superiors. That's helpful right? We swear we're not trying to shortcut things.

But in all seriousness, management decides what each employee's schedule looks like, based on the needs of the company. As a manager, being proactive to find or develop answers to these questions, then exercising your leadership skills by being transparent and forthcoming with that information, will go a long way in making your team a well-oiled, happy machine.

The Long Answer

Now for the longer answer. There isn't a one-size-fits-all formula for what a typical nine-to-five workday even looks like—notwithstanding the reminder that it's a fairly American idea to begin with and as such should be thought of as a cultural thing and not a universal thing. It's going to be different for every organization based on their needs.

If your company sets work hours from 9 a.m. to 5 p.m. in the time zone in which the headquarters is located, that's fine. Or work hours might be set from 9 a.m. to 5 p.m. in whatever time zone the employee is located. Or perhaps it allows for a completely flexible work schedule, which is set by each individual employee (see the next chapter for more on this type of work day).

> *I lived in Virginia and managed teams in Japan and Australia. That meant 2 a.m. conference calls and a schedule that had to be bent to fit the client. My colleagues in Fairfax couldn't understand why I was sleepy at our 9 a.m. staff meetings. I finally adjusted my hours and worked 5 p.m. to 2 a.m., which was just enough overlap with the Fairfax team. Our clients often didn't realize that I was in the United States, which was always the highest compliment that I could get.*
>
> —Court Ogilvie, Consultant,
> Principal, Tenada Consulting Group

The more important point here is to make your expectations clear up front and document them. If the hours are 9 a.m.–5 p.m. in your headquarter city's time zone, than a virtual employee who lives in a time zone that's eight hours ahead will need to understand that this is a requirement of the job and be agreeable to it. If there is a little wiggle room within those parameters and it's within your power to make accommodations, work with the staff member to figure out what that looks like. At the end of the day, you need to make sure that your staff is crystal clear on what is expected of them as far as their work hours are concerned, and then sign off that they understand. This management skill will serve you in both virtual- and stationary-based management settings and cannot be overstated.

Nine-to-Five Management in a Global Workplace

OK, at this point you're probably saying "Thanks for all of this, but the real issue is how do I best manage people in *my* nine-to-five while dealing with any number of nine-to-five realities around the world?"

For starters you need to do it thoughtfully. This includes gaining the full support of your company when it comes to setting expectations for your time, your employees' needs, and the needs of the company.

You'll also want to be more flexible when it comes to dealing with immediate or crucial issues from direct reports. You know how many companies offer flex time for work travel, attending conferences, or attending or setting up events? This is no different. If you need to spend one or more days a week working "off hours" for one employee who is 12 hours off your schedule on a short- or long-term project or assignment, you might ask to shift your hours elsewhere. It's not only fair, it's reasonable to ensure you're doing your job well with your entire team on everyone's time, not just your own.

A Few More Thoughts

✓ Track your team's schedule. Take out a piece of paper or create a grid! You'll all benefit if you can see what everyone's typical work schedule looks like individually, as well as how it overlaps collectively. Use your chart to visualize how everyone can and can't work "together" when necessary.

> *I have worked in the virtual team environment on a global scale for the last 10 years. This not only involved regularly leading meetings across varying time zones, holidays, and language barriers, but also understanding how to effectively gather information and communicate expectations cross-culturally and within local regulations. You cannot expect to (virtually) march into an office half a world away and assume you understand what process improvements need to be put into place solely based on the fact that you all fall under the same corporate umbrella.*
>
> *In the beginning—and as we added new countries to our scope of work—I was repeatedly caught off-guard by the vast differences in readily available technical resources, means of electronic communication, and the level of governmental engagement in daily processes, as well as the sheer extent of things I take for granted. The virtual workplace has given us extensive access to one another and opportunities to collaborate on new solutions to issues we all face in trying to create consistent customer experiences and seamless business practices. This environment literally puts the world at our fingertips while exponentially expanding our depth of perspective.*
>
> —Jennie Adamik, Global Brokerage Training Specialist
> With an International Supply Chain Provider

✓ **Convert the chart to all relevant time zones;** for example, if your employee is in Singapore, create a Singapore chart. This will help you look like a rock star to your international colleagues and prove that you are truly interested in being as inclusive as possible.

✓ **Share this chart.** If someone's trying to schedule a conference call, this graph would be ideal because it allows them to see where the workday overlaps so they can make the best scheduling choices possible.

✓ **Track your own hours.** Sometimes trying to lead a global team with any intimacy is difficult. When it's proving to be so, and your hours start exponentially expanding, you need to talk with your supervisor about the realities of leading a global team remotely.

✓ **Remain open minded.** There may come a point where the established schedule no longer works for your international employee. Make sure your lines of communication are open and they can come to you to discuss potential schedule adjustments. This will not only show them that they are a valuable asset to your organization, but also reinforce your openness as a virtual manager.

Signing Off

In a virtual world, nine-to-five can be a workplace norm that becomes very abnormal very quickly. Ultimately, the hours an employee works are determined by their supervisor (or those even higher in some instances) and they're going to be different based on organizational needs. If your hours are strict, they're strict. If they are flexible, they're flexible. If set hours are nonexistent, they're nonexistent. Whatever your company policy is, it just needs to be clearly communicated to your staff—no matter what time zone they work in.

3.

How to Address and Accommodate a Flexible Schedule

Who doesn't love the idea of a 15-second commute to our home office, or being able to work in our most comfortable clothes? One of the things that we and many other virtual employees love best about working virtually is the possibility of a *flexible schedule,* or the ability to work inside or outside the typical nine-to-five as desired.

As with other topics in this book, you must decide what works best for your organization. Perhaps that includes flexible schedules. But going a little deeper, what might that look like for your workplace and especially your team?

Let's Level Set, Shall We?

One of the themes you'll see us touch on again and again is how the virtual workplace is a reflection of the modern workplace. This is no more true than when talking about flexible schedules. Not only are most online businesses technically open 24/7, but even brick-and-mortar businesses are feeling the pressure to include flexibility in how they interact with and offer services to customers and clients. The standard nine-to-five universe is shrinking, and that means our expectations to push anyone into those timeframes—employees or anyone else—must change too.

These days, offering flexible schedules is more about meeting organizational needs, rather than just accommodating someone's interest in working when they want. When the work needs to get done, it often just needs to get done. And we're afraid that doesn't always fall into the traditional nine-to-five timeframe. Does this mean you should always be on? Or that you should expect your employees to be at the ready at all times? Not at all. But it does mean that you need to consider flexibility as part of the job, not just a perk.

> *Working with people all over the globe definitely requires a good bit of flexibility. It's nice when things can be handled over email, but sometimes a phone call or video conference is necessary to get the job done. When I have had to meet with someone in a different time zone at a time that was outside my normal nine-to-five, I have been fortunate enough to be able to flex or slide my schedule to meet that demand. So, if I had a 9 p.m. phone call my time, I could either slide my schedule to work two-to-ten rather than nine-to-five, or I could work my normal schedule, take the evening call, and then start work an hour later the next day.*
>
> *—Kathy*

Time to Flex Your Hours

There is no hard and fast definition for what flexibility should look like in the workplace—barring that it's necessary to conduct a larger flow of work that's more global in nature—so it is up to you and those above you to figure out how it works and, as always, back those decisions up with your policies and procedures. Flexible scheduling can manifest in three different ways with room to mix and match—limited flexibility, moderate flexibility, and full flexibility.

Let's look at a couple of examples of how different levels of flexibility might work and discuss a few tips for working within each framework. Perhaps this will spark some ideas for how you can incorporate flexibility as effectively as possible into your environment.

Limited Flexibility

One way to set up a limited flexibility workplace is to set core business or working hours and then allow staff to slide on either side. For example, if your company sets six standard hours of expected set time, your core hours might be 10 a.m. to 4 p.m. During this time, all employees are required to be working; however, they can slide their schedules however they like on either side. So, employees who like to get up early can work 8 a.m.–4 p.m. Others who like to sleep in a little may choose to work 10 a.m.–6 p.m. Employees who fit somewhere in the middle could work 9 a.m.–5 p.m. The flexibility is limited in that for those six core hours, everyone must be working, but the start and end times are theirs to schedule as they wish.

Isn't this just a modern version of having shifts? Not if you're the kind of company that needs 24-hour operations that require employees to work in set shifts around the clock. However, if you need people 24/7, you can set four to six hours of time in shift models, but allow your employees to decide how to manage the other two to four hours of their day. Now we're talking about flexibility again set to the tune of standards.

You can also add another layer of flexibility within this setup. For example, can people change their hours daily, depending on what is going on in their lives? Can they work 8 a.m.–4 p.m. one day and 10 a.m.–6 p.m. the next? Do they need permission?

This is a good way to test the waters of flexibility. You can start here and see if it works for your company. Or maybe try a trial run on Mondays or Fridays to get the ball rolling. You can be flexible about how flexible your schedules are. We know, it's very meta.

Moderate Flexibility

Moderate flexibility could be giving employees the ability to choose their work hours without any core hours in place, as long as they're still working Monday through Friday. Additionally, they must understand that meetings will be scheduled at the discretion of management, and all staff are required to attend, regardless of their regularly chosen schedule.

With moderate flexibility one employee might work 8 a.m.–4 p.m., while another chooses to work 12 p.m.–8 p.m. Or someone could split their day—work 8 a.m.–2 p.m., take a break to get their kids off the bus and make dinner, and then work again from 6 p.m. to 8 p.m. every night. However, to our point earlier, if you call a standing meeting every Tuesday at 11 a.m., even the employee who works 12 p.m.–8 p.m. has to be "at work" by 11 a.m. Tuesdays, no questions asked.

This flexibility provides staff with much greater auton- omy over their work lives, but still ties everyone to a standard unification of structure. It also lets folks take a stronger approach to managing their work and life balance—something that is often touted as one of the main benefits of working virtually.

Full Flexibility

Full flexibility is the grand prize of the flexibility game! If you are a full flexibility business, you allow your staff to work whenever they chose, as long as they put in their full 40 hours and complete the work assigned to them. One recommendation we would make, however, is that this level of flexibility be reserved for mature, established teams made of staff you know can handle this much flexibility and who have demonstrated capability with a work ethic to match. This benefit is best utilized with those you know are going to get the job done.

If you're considering implementing full flexibility in your organization, you may want to phase it in. For example, start with full flexibility every Monday, Wednesday, and Friday, but only moderate flexibility on Tuesdays and Thursdays for the first few months. This will help everyone get their bearings.

Although there is great satisfaction, independence, and freedom in working virtually, I think it's important to note that we are all better together than alone. As independent contractors, we share knowledge collectively and use the experiences of our clients around the globe to learn more and help them avoid risk. Being tied to a "mother ship" like Maritz allows me to tap into resources that might otherwise make me feel like I had one hand tied behind my back.

—Mimi Whitney, National Account Manager,
Experient—a Maritz Global Events Company

A Few More Thoughts

✓ **Keep time zones in mind.** If people on your team live in varying time zones, you have to keep this in mind when developing your plan for workplace flexibility. In fact, it might force a kind of universal flexibility in how you manage your own schedule to help support all of your direct reports.

✓ **Create benchmarks and deadlines.** To test your flexibility plan, develop benchmarks and deadlines to help measure the effectiveness of flexible work time. How? Flexibility makes people happy. Happy people are more productive and get their work done. If they are meeting their deadlines and doing good work, your flexibility plan is effective!

✓ **Don't equate fairness with sameness.** This tip might be a little controversial, but stick with us for a second. There may come a time that you realize it doesn't make sense for a certain position to be flexible. Notice we said *position*, not *person*. Let's say you're the president or CEO and you choose to work strictly 9 a.m. to 5 p.m. You've probably got an executive assistant that you spend a lot of time working closely with. Or perhaps your company has positions that work in in customer service, requiring a set timeframe for answering calls each and every day. It might not make good business sense to offer flexible schedules for these positions. In these cases, it's important to make those expectations clear up front so your staff can decide for themselves if this is the right fit for them. Be open and disclose the fact that while other staff have flexible schedules, this particular position is not conducive to that.

✓ **Tout flexibility as a perk.** Flexible work schedules can be particularly helpful in nonprofit organizations where bosses are often looking for ways to offer perks, but may not have the money for other costly benefits. If you're used to running a tight ship, but are considering implementing flexibility, start with the limited flexibility option and see how it goes. If all goes well, advance to moderate flexibility and perhaps even full flexibility later on.

Signing Off

Flexible schedules are a fantastic perk, but they're also often necessary to get work done today. Either way, allowing staff to choose their own schedules is a great, no-cost benefit. However, you need to make sure it's part of your policies, procedures, and culture—flexibility without reliability and definition is the gateway to instability.

And remember, these are just a few of the ways you can experiment with flexibility. What other ways can you dream up? The flexibility world is your oyster, there for the exploring for both personnel perks and pragmatic business practices. But we assure you—flexibility is not just the future—it's now. And giving your staff the flexibility to balance their work and personal lives is a benefit that reaches far beyond what you will ever be able to see. It makes for happy, satisfied employees and can even contribute to your employees' overall wellness. And who doesn't want that?

4.

How to
Ensure Privacy

The topic of technology and privacy is top of mind for just about everyone. Topics such as digital data transfer, password security, cloud storage vulnerability, and even how often we share personal photos and information on social media can keep anyone up at night. And that's just the tip of the iceberg.

So how privacy plays into the topic of virtual employment is not only paramount, but heavily layered. It might be easy to assume that the responsibility of ensuring privacy is first and foremost that of the employer. But we would argue that an employee plays an equally crucial part in securing their personal interests as well as the privacy interests of the client or company. In fact, while we're quick to generically blame technology for breaches in issues related to privacy, the truth is that the number 1 interest in breaching privacy is a human one and is almost always initiated by humans.

Let's Level Set, Shall We?

In a modern sense, what does it mean to "ensure privacy" as a virtual manager and for virtual employees? In brief, it means many things, including considerations, necessary policies, and safeguards. In other chapters, we tackle a wealth of funny, weird, and all-too-common privacy-related topics that employees and employers deal with in a virtual world. However to kick things off, we're going to first address privacy at a fundamental level for you and your employees.

Understanding the Vulnerabilities of Your Tech

It's a safe bet that the majority of the technology you and your team use comes from your employer—everything from your computer to the docking station, phone to router. Most companies handle all of the software and hardware necessary for your day-to-day job.

No matter who supplies your tech, you still need to protect it to the best of your ability. We've compiled some classic privacy and security tips for you and those who report to you to remember at all times.

Password Protect Everything

If your password is PASSWORD1 or 1234ABCD or even some combo of your child's first name and date of birth—*spoiler alert*—you're a security hazard. We understand that remembering passwords is hard, so one of the best things you can do is use the complex auto-generated passwords that are offered to you by your computer. If you write them down, keep them in a safe and secure place (not scribbled on a piece of paper "hidden" underneath your keyboard). There are also online password storage platforms that offer to safely store all your passwords in one place, but beware that even these can be compromised by the savviest of hackers.

Keep Your Computer Updated and Virus Free

Stop ignoring virus and update notifications! Of course they are annoying. Of course they pop up in the middle of working on a late report. And of course they take a lot of time exactly when you don't have it. But every time you click on "remind me later" you're not really hitting "snooze"—you're leaving your computer open to any number of attacks. Sometimes it's hard to tell if these notifications are real or not. That's when you take a screenshot from your desktop and send it to IT to ensure you should be updating what you're being asked to update—assuming IT doesn't handle all of this already anyway without you even knowing.

Use or Request a Virtual Private Network (VPN)

These days, most organizations with a sizeable virtual employee base use a VPN regularly. VPNs allow you to connect to the Internet through a remote (or virtual) server. As a result, the data sent between your device and this server is securely encrypted and gives you privacy by hiding your Internet behavior from both your ISP and any other group that may be tracking your browsing information. VPNs are also smart because they can be used to open access to blocked websites or restrict other websites, based on what your company does or does not want you to access.

Use Only Secure Wi-Fi Networks

While the free Wi-Fi service at your local Starbucks or Panera seems super convenient when you're working remotely, recall the little message that pops up about how your private information may not be private on their network? Can't remember? Our point exactly. Because when you use public Wi-Fi, anyone could be watching both literally and digitally. And if you're using public Wi-Fi for work, you want to take an extra set of security measures, such as using a VPN service to encrypt any data you send or installing an encrypted private hotspot for added security.

Secure Your Browsers

Your browser is how you interact with the virtual world, and if you're not careful, it's easy to leave a trail of digital footprints everywhere you go, which subsequently leaves you open to trackers and hackers checking out your private browsing habits. It's become harder and harder to turn off third-party cookies, but where you can, you need to block them. Going a step further, it's also worth disabling JavaScript to avoid hackers. And nowadays, it's not a bad idea to turn on all of your browser privacy settings anyway, keeping your work computer clean from any vulnerable website.

Understanding the Vulnerabilities of Your Actions

Technology is one place you need to lock down your securities and privacies, but your actions—and the actions of those who report to you—are another issue all together. Privacy is a multi-lane highway. Do you know what side you and your employees are on?

One of the first places you should look is to see if your company has any expectations or restrictions for how you use your tech. But just to be safe, we've got you covered with a few smart tips.

Use Company-Required Security Measures

It's likely that your company expects you to use a confidentiality statement in your email signature, or that it has a firewall policy related to online computer usage. No matter what the requirements are, follow all of them. They are there for a reason and are often the first line of defense against breaks in confidentiality.

Avoid Creating Email Chains or Reply-Alls

You have one of two choices when replying to an email chain: Read the entire email chain again to ensure you're not creating any confidential jeopardy by hitting reply all, or don't continue the chain and simply reply directly to the sender. Otherwise you are leaving the whole thing ripe for mistakes. And we've all been there.

Mark It Confidential

Confidential workplace information can generally be broken down into three categories: employee information, management information, and business information. In a virtual world, one of the best things you can do when dealing with a private or confidential issue is to make sure that before the person involved even opens, accepts, or is engaged in the conversation, they are made aware of its confidential or private nature. Don't assume that the sheer nature of the topic should alert someone to its confidentiality. Give them a heads-up to ensure you're all on the same page. How can you accomplish this? It can be as easy as writing "Confidential" in the subject line of the email or invite. We also recommend taking several precautions when planning to address confidential or private issues on a video or phone call, virtually.

Keep Your Work Computer Professional

Don't use social media, conduct personal searches, or shop retail on your work computer. It's tempting. We know! It's just another tab away! And it's the modern world, right? Who cares if you're on Facebook or Amazon over lunch? Or that you jump on LinkedIn to connect with a colleague? Resist the urge.

Unless managing social media or ordering office supplies is part of your job description, use your personal phone, watch, tablet, or other device to check on your newsfeed, search for the closest pizza delivery, or order a new pair of jeans. The possibilities of inviting problems—professional or technical—are far too high to risk using work tech for the purpose of personal needs.

A Few More Thoughts

✓ **Make privacy a priority.** Privacy is more than just an issue for employers. It's an issue for everyone involved, and this means that everyone needs to be involved at all levels that relate to their role.

✓ **Keep up to date on privacy issues.** In a virtual environment, knowing more is always better than knowing less or knowing where to point someone. Learn what you can about confidentiality, privacy, and protections, and pass that information on to help make everyone who reports to you feel smart, confident, and compliant.

Signing Off

We cannot reinforce enough how critically important privacy is in a modern virtual world. A breach of information is not just an "oops" occurrence. In fact, with the General Data Protection Regulations (GDPR) that went into effect in Europe in early 2018, indiscretion when it comes to privacy could potentially result in fines that reach into the millions of euros—not exactly something for which you want to be personally responsible!

A lot of the information presented in this chapter was pretty "techy," and that may not be your area of expertise. Therefore, our suggestion would be to talk to your IT person so they can make sure the devices you use for work are as protected as they can be. Take all topics of privacy seriously and utilize any and all precautions. If you see something and don't know whether it's real or if you should click on it, ask someone immediately. It's totally OK to take the "there's no shame in my game" attitude and get things checked out. Remember, once information is breached, it cannot be unbreached, so be vigilant—even when it's annoying. Like with most things, it's better to be safe than sorry. And in the virtual world, it even better to be very safe than sorry you didn't try harder.

THE NEW VHR

Handling Virtual
Human Resources
and Team
Management

5.

Hiring and Interviews

When bringing on new staff members, we always set out to find the best person for the job—that's a given. This philosophy shouldn't change when searching for virtual employees. But don't be fooled! The knowledge, skills, and abilities you're looking for and the questions you ask during the interview process will, by default, be a little bit different for a virtual employee. In this chapter, we're here to tell you how to do it right!

Let's Level Set, Shall We?

Hiring a new employee can be hard—and time consuming. And while it's often the job of HR staff and recruiters to tackle much of the initial interview process before the manager is brought in, we recommend you make sure that everything is in order—especially if you don't have that initial HR support. As with any hiring decision, you need an approved job description, a job ad, and a place to put that ad. You also need to develop the interview questions. Then, you need to keep up with all the incoming resumes. It is a process that costs a lot of time and money. But throw a virtual hire into that mix and, well, you have a whole new set of things to consider to make the placement as successful as possible.

It's kind of like a recipe for banana bread that you've been making all your life, and suddenly you want to make it for someone who is gluten free. It's still the same basic recipe, but the flour needs to be switched out and replaced with several different ingredients to make the banana bread as delicious as usual. All the typical qualifications for the open position need to be in place, but there are also some additional things to consider that we will talk about here. In this case, the gluten-free flour is hosting meetings on camera, and while you're not going to suddenly add nuts to the mix, you do need to make sure virtual candidates know how to use email and shared document systems effectively. You know, that kind of stuff.

I remember the first person I interviewed virtually. It was with a massive national organization, so HR set up the initial details, complete with links to the video portal service we used and instructions for the candidate to test her video equipment. The candidate was also sent the organization's philosophy on why we conduct on-camera interviews for remote employees.

At the start of the interview her camera was off. "Are you having problems turning on your camera?" I asked. "No," she replied simply. "We prefer to interview candidates on camera for remote roles," I started. "Well, I'm interviewing for a virtual job so I don't have to be on camera or get dressed for work every day," she said, cutting me off. It was a very short interview. I don't know what happened to her virtual employment goals, but I hope wherever she landed, she's happy, healthy, and showered.

—Ben

Seek, and Ye Shall Find
(If You Know What You're Looking For)

The idea of virtual employment is still somewhat novel when compared to the overall workforce. While it's the fastest growing version of employment, there is still an overwhelming number of people who have never had the opportunity to work virtually. But because it has so many benefits, virtual positions are desired by job seekers both with and without virtual work experience.

What does this mean for you? It is extra important during the interview process to look for clues that a candidate might just be looking for an opportunity to work from home, and listen for evidence that the aptitudes to work virtually successfully are present.

So what should you be looking for in a virtual employee? This is where it all begins. Right here, right now, it is imperative that you get clear on what you are looking for in a virtual employee that will make them a good fit for the constitution and culture of your organization. These are things that we cannot spell out for you—only *you* are going to know.

Beyond the culturally specific details of your organization, certain skills and aptitudes will go a long way toward a successful virtual placement. Have you ever seen a thread sticking out on a sweater? Did you pull it? Don't worry—this is a judgment-free zone. At first you thought you would quickly come to the end of it, but then it kept pulling, and so did you, until you realized the impact that little thread had on your sweater as a whole.

So it is with the specific attributes that we're going to discuss. They may seem basic, but their absence could have huge implications for the culture, community, effectiveness, and productivity of your team. These attributes include:

- technological savvy and flexibility
- excellent communication skills on various mediums
- independent drive and ambition
- self-discipline
- self-starting and self-motivation.

Technological Savvy and Flexibility

In this world of ever-changing, fast-paced technology, it doesn't matter what industry you're in, you need to be able to keep up and learn new tech and updated tech with certain levels of success. This is not news. But in the virtual workplace, this is where and how the work is completed. You need people who can roll with the technological punches. We all know that an IT expert can be necessary for those tougher, more complicated fixes. However, when working in a virtual environment, it is so helpful and time saving for everyone if the employee can at least find their way around their computer, their Wi-Fi, and the platforms that you use within your organization for project management and communication.

Luckily, computers have been around long enough that it's getting rarer and rarer to find people who don't at least have a working knowledge of computers and basic office-oriented operating systems, and have the ability to find their way around cables, hardware, printer issues, and so forth. And those who cannot probably aren't applying for a virtual position to begin with.

To determine a candidate's technological aptitude, go ahead and ask questions along these lines during the interview:

- What steps do you take when you get a message that your printer is offline?
- What happens if your VPN isn't working?
- How would you handle getting the "blue screen of death"?

- Do you have experience with the project management platform the organization has adopted? If not, how would you go about getting up to speed on it?
- How would you handle the inevitable situation of changing technology, upgrades, and the like?
- Do you know how to set up group invitations for a meeting in a calendar system?
- Where is your threshold between troubleshooting the problem yourself and calling IT?

The answers to these questions and more are important because working virtually is 100 percent dependent on computers. A virtual environment certainly makes IT issues more of a challenge, so you want someone who can hold their own in this space. And if IT is needed, the candidate needs to be knowledgeable enough to have an IT person walk them through the steps necessary to fix the problem. Because the IT person? Yeah, they're probably virtual too.

Excellent Communication Skills on Various Mediums

Being able to communicate clearly in any setting or situation, let alone a virtual work environment, is imperative. An employee who is working virtually should understand the importance of good communication and possess a demonstrated proficiency on a variety of mediums. When overseeing a virtual team, you have little room for miscommunication, so it is your job when hiring a new staff member to ensure your candidate's ability. How can you do this? Obviously you can pick up on some of this in the early stages before you ever meet the person. Review their resume and cover letter. Are they well written? Do they communicate key points about their knowledge, skills, and abilities? Did they take care in the production of their materials, using complete sentences free from spelling and grammatical errors? These are all good initial indicators. But let's take it even further.

It is perfectly acceptable to request a writing sample from your candidates, especially if writing—whether formally with clients and constituents or informally within your team—is a major part of the job. And we can assure you—in a virtual work environment, it is. You can even place parameters around this request regarding type of writing, length, and medium. Ask for a sample that aligns with the position for which you are interviewing. Is the job heavy on social media? Ask for a sample post on email and via text. Is it a grant-writing position? Ask for a sample grant narrative. One tip here would be to make sure your request is reasonable; don't ask for a dissertation. And if possible, ask for the writing sample in advance, like when you set up the interview date, that way the candidate has some time to think about it or to find a real-life sample of work they have done.

But writing isn't the only form of communication virtual employees use. You should be able to pick up on the interviewee's verbal communication skills by listening to or watching them answer your interview questions. But sometimes you may want to take it a step further. For example, if it's a customer service position, you may want to work in a short role play of a call with a disgruntled customer to see how they communicate when under a little pressure.

Another interesting option here is to give them a scenario in advance of the interview, and ask them to prepare a short presentation to give on camera during the interview process. This will allow you to see their presentation and verbal communication skills at the same time.

Now is the absolute best time to think outside the box!

> *There is one particular virtual interview I remember that really sticks out to me. The position was a stationary one, but the interviewee was traveling and could not physically come into the office for the interview, so we conducted it via online video conferencing. This was a great way to get to see the candidate and have her see us. There were a few technical glitches along the way but it was nice to be able to watch her take these glitches in stride and remain focused on the interview. We were able to see her personality and her ability to roll with the punches shine through, and she was the candidate that we ended up hiring.*
>
> —Kathy

How you figure out the depth of a candidate's communication skills is really up to you. Just make sure you do it and use a variety of virtual office technologies. Be observant of words, tone, and body language (because if you can't interview in person, you're conducting it on camera, right?). Being able to communicate appropriately and build relationships in a virtual environment is absolutely necessary.

Independent Drive and Ambition

In our virtual world, an ideal candidate will be filled with drive—something we understand may seem very abstract and a difficult attribute to detect. So let's take a deeper dive. Someone who is independently driven has a certain energy, and is ambitious and results-oriented without needing to be told they should have those attributes. During the interview process look for stories about how the candidate previously headed up a project, organized it, and propelled it through to completion. Not only that, but look for their level of excitement when telling the story. Do they seem eager to share the story? Are they keen to explain the results of that project, or how it led to another project and more great results? These could be good indicators of independent drive.

And drive matters because in a virtual environment people often work more independently than not, even if it's more felt than real. Someone might not be any more connected, watched, or prompted in a stationary workplace than a virtual one, but the feeling of being more connected, watched, or prompted is often part of that office environment, unlike the virtual workplace.

Independently driven people tend to be very results-oriented. They are extremely interested in the end game and ensuring that they hit the mark on what they set out to do—both inside and outside what's expected of them. This excites them and helps them feel fulfilled in their position. If you can sense this excitement oozing from them as they tell you stories of past accomplishments, it is a very good sign. The driven person is not only interested in what a position can do for them, but also what they can make of the position and the goals and objectives that come with it. This candidate will show an understanding of what your needs are and be eager to fill them. Making the organization look good makes them feel good. These are great qualities to have in your new staff member.

Self-Discipline

Virtual employees need to be self-disciplined. Your virtual employees are not under constant supervision—and shouldn't have to be, because you've chosen the very best person for the job and we're all adults here, right? Working throughout the day for your entire "shift" as if you were in an office setting is obviously the right and ethical thing to do, but it can be a challenge if someone lacks self-discipline—especially those who are working from home for the very first time. It's tempting to see something around the house that needs to be done and then get up to do it. We've all seen those memes about going to put something away, only to find dust on the shelf, so you go to get a rag to clean off the dust, but on the way you see dirty dishes in the sink and stop to wash them, and before you know it you don't remember what you got up to do or why. Without self-discipline, virtual employees can easily lose several hours of their day being distracted by other things that need to be done in their environment, rather than the work on their desktops.

Of course, self-discipline is also very difficult to sniff out in an interview. But not impossible. Here are some tips:

- Ask the candidate if they have ever worked virtually before and what kept them on track during the day.
- If they haven't worked virtually before, ask them how they intend to practice self-discipline to get the job done.
- Ask for an example of how they have exhibited self-discipline in their life, whether personally or professionally. If they are an avid runner, for example, and wake up at 4:30 a.m. every day to make sure they get in a three- to five-mile run before work, rain or shine, they are probably very self-disciplined.

The candidate's answers will help you see if they are self-disciplined. Listen for clues that the person is structured or follows a specific routine. Ask about their work processes or procedures for organizing priorities. A person who is self-disciplined will have quick answers to these questions, because it's how they live their life.

Self-Starting and Self-Motivation

While discipline focuses on doing what is right even when you don't want to, motivation is the "want to" in the first place. It's the reason behind the choice you make to do something—the stimulus or impetus.

Some great questions to ask to get to the heart of a candidate's self-starting nature are:

- What is your biggest professional accomplishment, and how did this accomplishment come to pass?
- What do you dream about?
- What goals have you set for yourself and how are you working to achieve them?
- After 30, 60, and 90 days on the job, how would you know you were successful?
- What does success look like to you?
- What motivates you to go the extra mile?

People who are self-motivated are not scared of putting in the work it's going to take to get to where they want to go. They keep their eye on the prize and have a vision of exactly how to get there. Oh, and obstacles? Not a problem! Self-motivated people anticipate obstacles and know the self-talk they need to move past them and keep on keeping on.

So, self-motivation gets to the core of why someone has the drive that they do, while self-discipline is their ability to do something no matter what their motivation—and if you can find these twin sisters in a job candidate, you have hit the mother lode! And if you find someone who also has their little brother, drive and ambition, you've most definitely found a unicorn! This person will be unstoppable. Scoop them up and never let them go!

Conducting the Interview

There are a number of ways to conduct interviews for a virtual candidate: email, phone, video, and in-person. Any or all are smart ways to learn how they thrive or struggle with virtual technologies and experiences. So let's break them down a bit and offer our thoughts on each to you as a manager.

Written/Email

Beyond the application, cover letter, and resume, there are a variety of ways to use the written word as part of the formal interview process. Asking candidates to respond to questions via email or in a written template or form is a great way to see how they write and carry themselves in print. The written word is often used heavily no matter the work environment, but it's used the most in virtual environments, because email and messaging are key facets of the modern workplace. So consider using more written options when conducting some of the early phases of the interview process, as opposed to just doing a phone interview.

Phone

In the stationary workplace, the phone interview is usually the first layer of knowing you're moving up the candidate pipeline. A phone interview is a great way to get to know someone in a more interpersonal way—it lets you hear their tone, their sense of humor, and how they react and respond to questions and insights. But as we said, phone interviews are often the entry-point for stationary environments because everyone knows an in-person interview is coming. The same can't be said for virtual environments. So while the phone interview is great, it shouldn't be the end-all-be-all of the virtual interview model. That honor should be reserved for video.

Video

By the end of this book, we will have either converted you to being a believer in video, or you will forever shudder when someone says "video chat." But video is ideal for the virtual world for a million little reasons—so much so that we cover it in just about every chapter. And the interview process is a great place to carry a more interpersonal dialogue about the candidate's goals, needs, hopes, and questions about your organization and their interests. It's also a great time to actually test their Wi-Fi a little, see how they conduct themselves virtually, and gain a little insight into their work or home life.

In Person

If you can, it's never a bad idea to interview someone in person. Virtual employment doesn't auto-exempt you from this option or its value. Is it necessary or essential? No. But in-person interviews can be great experiences for everyone involved and should always be on the table if possible.

No matter how you conduct your interviews, we recommend using a mix of the mediums. Considering how much of your new employee's experience will also leverage those mediums, the interview process is the absolute hands-down best place to begin learning how a candidate conducts themselves with these forms of engagement. Better to learn early, rather than after making an offer, that someone hates being on camera or doesn't write well outside of their (possibly outsourced) cover letter.

A Few More Thoughts

✓ **Picture perfection.** Prepare for your interviews by really thinking through what you're looking for in your next successful placement. You won't be able to find what you need if you don't know what you're looking for.

✓ **Why virtual?** Listen carefully during interviews and try to deduce the real reason someone wants to work from home. If they focus completely or mostly on how it will benefit them personally, it might not be a good fit. In fact, it's perfectly acceptable to ask them point blank why they want to work from home, and you might want to do this as early in the interview as possible.

✓ **Look for trust.** Humans tend to be pretty good at reading other humans. In a virtual environment, you have to be able to build trust with your staff. You can often begin to figure out if a trusting relationship will be achievable during the initial interview process.

✓ **Trust your gut.** If you see any kind of red flag in a candidate, even if it's a tiny flag, and it feels like it wouldn't be a good placement, it's probably not. As a manager, you need to have enough confidence in yourself to trust your instincts and pass on candidates who don't feel like a good match, whether it's because of skill set, culture, or one of the five key attributes mentioned in this chapter. And then, don't feel guilty about it! It is better to continue your search and find the right person. Think about the alternative—if you don't listen to your gut and hire someone who was not exactly what you were looking for, you could find yourself right back at the interview table before too long, looking to fill the position again, which costs time and money.

✓ **Virtual isn't for everyone.** If you do happen to hire someone that doesn't work out for any reason, don't feel guilty or place the blame completely on yourself. These things happen. It is what it is. Just take what you can from the experience, roll with the punches, and keep pressing on.

Signing Off

If you want the very best virtual employees, you have to look for more than just the skills outlined in a typical position description. You have to look for someone who can and does go a little further, who is a little more independent, and who really wants to be and do more than is expected. Be sure to look for the five key attributes listed in this chapter. The right candidate inherently brings these skills to the table and can do great things for your organization. But don't stop there. Remember—a job is a two-way street. When you're ready to make an offer, make sure it is competitive and appealing and that your perks and benefits make it the clear choice for the candidate. And how do you do that? Well, read on.

6.

Diversity, Inclusion, and Equity

The subjects of workplace diversity, inclusion, and equity are massive—often highly debated—issues in the workplace. And while we want to touch on each, we're not going to pretend you came here to learn about their core constructs, history, or progressive influences in our day-to-day work lives. Those are topics more effectively covered by other resources.

What we want to focus on is how the virtual workplace can create unintentional blind spots for deterring the work of diversity, inclusion, and equity. However, with the proper focus, you can serve to help the virtual workplace become more diverse, more inclusive, and more equitable. But it's going to take some insight and savvy to get us there.

Let's Level Set, Shall We?

It helps to start with what we mean by diversity, inclusion, and equity. Diversity in the work environment promotes acceptance, respect, and teamwork despite differences in race, age, gender, native language, political beliefs, religion, sexual orientation, or communication styles among employees. Inclusion is the action or state of effectively including everyone employed within a group or structure. And equity is about the quality of being fair and impartial with all employees equally. The exciting thing is that, assuming someone is comfortable with technology utilization and adoption, the virtual workplace often levels the playing field when it comes to issues of diversity, and highlights the power technology can play with inclusion and equity.

Diversity in the Virtual Workplace

As a virtual manager, managing virtual employees, do you know what your needs are? In a classic stationary workplace, when it comes to diversity, it's not too difficult to address and build a workforce that resembles the community where it resides. But in a virtual environment, the template that allows for a more casual "community of reflection" is a bit more complicated.

The virtual workplace allows your candidate pool to be global in nature. This allows you to dramatically increase candidate pipelines, experiences, and backgrounds (assuming you play a role in hiring your team), which then allows for diversity in your candidate screenings. There are a few tools you can use to assist this, such as:

- **Pre-hire assessments.** These are tests or questionnaires that candidates complete as part of their application process. Pre-hire assessments are often considered effective ways to determine which applicants are the most qualified for a specific job based on their strengths and preferences. They often help increase workplace diversity because personality scores do not significantly differ for any category of minority group members. However, it's important to refrain from asking about a candidate's personal background, age, race, gender, or ethnicity to avoid creating any unnecessary bias. In fact, we'd suggest that you apply a "blind hiring" process to ensure you're not creating unnecessary bias.

- **Blind hiring.** Usually aided by a technology tool, blind hiring is a technique that makes a candidate anonymous from a recruiter or hiring manager so that unconscious or conscious bias about the candidate can be averted. Similar to the pre-hire assessment model, this allows the candidate to be reviewed with their core skills and experiences as the primary focus.

Inclusion and Equity in the Virtual Workplace

It doesn't matter who you are or where you are, or your race, age, gender, native language, political beliefs, religion, sexual orientation, disability status, or communication styles—the virtual workplace isn't driven by knowing or needing those details. In fact, technology is growing so fast that most gaps caused by diversity attributes (such as a disability, native language, or communication styles) can be effectively supported or narrowed by a wide variety of technological designs. Often known as D&I technologies, these solutions use software and hardware to aid companies and employees with translation tools, disability and different-ability modifications to traditional software and hardware, and communication influencers to help support regional language and cultural nuances. These are powerful tools that can help the modern company grow their virtual landscape into a global workforce.

The note here for managers of virtual employees is knowing that the virtual workplace affords a wealth of advantages to help level the playing field for employees of all types and experiences. And while they're not magic, D&I technologies create a way to address issues such as workplace inclusion and equity with a fresh set of tools and approaches.

We're reminded of the great Martin Luther King Jr. quote, "Everybody can be great . . . because anybody can serve." It's a nice parallel allegory to how virtual employment can allow everyone to be great, because it allows anyone to work—no matter where, no matter how, no matter when.

But how does this happen? Magically? Nope. Just like the very technology virtual workers benefit from, the process of allowing for increased diversity, inclusion, and equity is done using a wealth of design and some well-crafted purpose.

Diversity, Inclusion, and Equity Flourish Under Virtual Employment

As stated by Meir Shemla (2018), associate professor for the department of organisation and personnel management at Rotterdam School of Management:

> Diversity gives you access to a greater range of talent, not just the talent that belongs to a particular worldview or ethnicity or some other restricting definition. It helps provide insight into the needs and motivations of all of your client or customer base, rather than just a small part of it. And, potentially, as McKinsey & Co and a host of other highly credible researchers have shown, it makes your organization more effective, more successful, more profitable.

Just as diverse talent isn't held to a specific worldview or ethnicity, neither is it held to the often noninclusive shackles of the stationary workplace. In the virtual workplace, work is more often evaluated and valued for what is expected and what is completed, not for how someone dresses in an interview or gets along in a cubicle setting. This is not to say that those facets of employment are lost on the virtual workplace—because they're not—but it does mean that the landscape of what diversity can offer and represents is both more amenable in the virtual workplace, while also being less prohibitive.

Say, for example, your stationary workplace doesn't include the best options for private places to pray or doesn't offer disability access to all parts of the building. In a virtual workplace, that's no longer an issue. These needs are accommodated virtually through access to one's own home or home office offerings. This is true too for populations like newly expecting or parents with babies and young children. While not every stationary workplace offers convenient or effective places for needs such as pumping, nursing, or general childcare, the virtual workplace is often a far more effective environment to meet these needs without needing permission, accommodation, or exceptions.

Your Role As a Virtual Manager

As a virtual manager, your role is to make these opportunities known and available to your virtual teams. While not always necessary, give your team permission to live the lives they need to live virtually. Even if your company doesn't offer formal benefits such as childcare subsidies or flexible schedules, tell your team that you're open to their needs and want to create a more inclusive and equitable workplace experience.

Let your team know you're willing to accommodate cultural and religious holidays, gender-reassignment needs, and diversity-friendly (but virtual office appropriate) apparel choices. The opportunities to learn more about how to best support all your employees are dramatically enhanced in the virtual workplace, so take full advantage.

A Few More Thoughts

✓ **Become a virtual leader for diversity and inclusion.** Take diversity management classes, read more on the subject, and engage with your employees more openly about their needs and experiences.

✓ **Create a culture of inclusion.** Create space for everyone to feel welcome in your virtual workplace. This starts in the outreach and application phase, continuing into the onboarding and training phase and your actions in the day-to-day as the manager.

✓ **Communicate the value of diversity and inclusion.** Make these topics core values within your management to express, learn, and grow. And make these values part of what you expect from your virtual teams as well.

✓ **Celebrate diversity and inclusion.** Beyond the culture and open communication, don't lose sight of all the ways you can celebrate diversity and increase inclusivity on your team where appropriate or necessary. Don't only look for ways to celebrate those on your team, but see how the technologies you leverage make for a more diverse and inclusive environment for everyone.

Signing Off

We are not just in an exciting time for virtual management and employment, we're also experiencing how virtual workplaces can offer more enhanced diversity, inclusion, and equity as a cultural norm. It's no secret that inclusive environments with diverse teams are more creative, accomplished, and have more open and effective communication. And as a virtual manager, you have to ask yourself how to create even more opportunities for these advantages to flourish under your leadership. And for that we are excited for you, and for all of us.

7.

Orientation and Onboarding

You've laughed, you've cried, you've worked hard reviewing resumes and interviewing, and you've hired the right person for the job. You have finally reached the finish line! It feels good to have done a successful job to increase the capacity of your team.

So now it pains us to burst your bubble and tell you that the finish line you thought you crossed was actually just another starting line. Because now it's time to onboard your new hire in a way that will set them up for success in your organization. But this isn't just any orientation—this is orientation for a virtual employee! You might be asking yourself, "Well, what's the difference?" and "How *can* I successfully onboard my new virtual employee?" We're glad you asked.

Let's Level Set, Shall We?

Orientation is not onboarding, but onboarding does involve

orientation. It's easy to get them mixed up, but they are truly two different things:

- **Onboarding** is an ongoing process of building employee engagement from the first contact until the employee becomes established within the organization. It can include a variety of training sessions, check-ins, meetings, and even evaluations.

- **Orientation** is often the earliest stage of onboarding, where new employees learn about the company, its culture, the basic rules, technologies, policies and procedures, and sometimes how their job responsibilities fit into the wider company.

As the manager, it is your job to make sure that everything within the orientation and onboarding process is done properly and thoroughly.

The More Things Change, the More They Stay the Same

It's worth noting that orientation and onboarding will be different for every organization because they depend on your company culture, policies, and procedures. While bringing on a proximity employee and a virtual employee may share many of the same elements, let's address some key differences. We'll cover each in more detail in other chapters, but this is a great place to talk about a few of the main nuances.

The new hire orientation is typically the first time new employees get a real taste for what it's like to work for your organization. This means that it's the best opportunity to make expectations clear and to set your new employee up for success. Many of these expectations are discussed and set during the interview process, but once the candidate is hired, those expectations become more relevant and real.

The new employee *wants* to learn what your organization is all about. They *want* to learn what is considered normal and acceptable within your employment culture. And most importantly, they *want* to be successful. If you approach this process with a partner mentality where you and your new employee are two members of the same team, you will lay the groundwork for the best possible employment situation for both parties.

So what exactly are the main differences in onboarding a proximity employee versus a remote employee? As we see it, there are two: The first and most obvious difference is that your remote employee is not someone you will see or necessarily interact with every day. And this presents some unique factors that need to be thoughtfully addressed during the orientation process. Second, it's quite possible in this situation that the orientation itself will take place remotely—although hopefully at least on camera—so your presentation style may have to be tweaked a bit to convey your messages thoroughly and appropriately.

Orientations for Remote Workers

What should you include in a remote employee orientation? As we've already touched on, one of the most important aspects to properly communicate is your organization's culture. Although the virtual world has been in existence for a few years now, some employers' movement into the virtual space is still somewhat slow. This means that working in a virtual environment is new to many in the workforce and needs to be personally socialized for them—which translates to lots of questions and unknowns surrounding culture. It is critical that you spend time thinking through how you present this piece of the orientation, as this will set the foundation for the new employee to feel like a well-informed, well-integrated part of the team.

You're going to want to start by picking apart the expectations and norms that you want to communicate to your new employee. Your employee handbook may cover these aspects, but they say we have to hear something seven times before it sticks. This is a good factoid to keep in mind. If it's important, go over it; then go over it again. Is the employee expected to be logged in to a specific program the entire day? Do you expect status buttons to be accurate and paid attention to? If the employee is hourly, how do they clock in and out? Are they expected to be on camera for meetings, or is it acceptable to use phone only? How long should their lunch break be? How do they indicate that they are at lunch so you know when not to call? All these things and more need to be taken into consideration when preparing an employee for remote work.

And there's more.

Remember when you graduated from high school and went off to college? It was probably the first time you were away from your parents, unsupervised. Did you get an overwhelming sense of freedom? Was it one of the most exciting times of your life? Well, landing a remote job (or moving to remote work in a current job) can feel a lot like going to college to people who have been in the workforce for a while and are experiencing work-from-home freedom for the first time. They know how to be a good employee—but do they know how to be a good employee from within the four walls of their own home? They most likely do, or you wouldn't have hired them or given them the opportunity to be remote. That said, they may need a little guidance and direction in the form of new-hire orientation and the setting of expectations right from the get go. Doing this properly and thoroughly and in a broader sense now will avoid the awkward situation later of having to address something the employee did that was considered wrong or unacceptable.

You're Disoriented on How to Orient

OK, you're all set. You've discussed with HR the elements that need to be considered in a virtual new hire orientation, you have your orientation ready, and it's appropriately catered to a virtual environment. The last step to making this sure this orientation hits the mark is figuring out *how* it will be presented.

The best way to handle a remote virtual orientation is using a conference call system that allows for camera usage (so you can see one another and interpret body language), as well as screen sharing so you can show any supporting slides. If you do not have access to a conference call system that provides both of these elements, you will have to make do. If this is the case, be sure to play up whichever aspect you have. If it's camera, try to be more animated and engaging because the information you're relaying can be somewhat dull. If you have just screen sharing, give your slide deck some color, flair, and excitement.

If you don't have any web conferencing capabilities, this would be a pickle, indeed. Not the end of the world, just a pickle. This might be a good time for you to attempt to exert some influence over the decision makers in your organization and suggest the importance of a service that does both video and screen sharing. Such a service will be extremely beneficial for all kinds of uses in the future—orientations, team meetings, presentations, trainings, and even disciplinary meetings—and is well worth the investment.

So what if you don't have any service, nor the budget or permission to purchase something? Well, we would recommend taking advantage of platforms that offer free, scaled down versions. They're not hard to find with a little Internet research.

And if all else fails, as a very last resort, send your new hire the slides, hop on the telephone, and go through the orientation letting them know when to change the slides. This is kind of archaic, but our point is that where there's a will, there's a way. And there should always be the will to provide an informative orientation. No matter what.

> More than a decade ago I was hired at a nonprofit to develop a volunteer program. The nature of this nonprofit was such that I didn't really have local, in-house volunteers. They were all virtual. This made my pool of potential volunteers so much wider, but also had its challenges, such as how to conduct orientations.
>
> At the time the volunteer program launched, we did not have a video conferencing service, so I PDFed all of my slides and emailed them to each new volunteer. I then held either group or one-on-one orientation sessions over the phone, conducting the orientation just as I would if they were in person. The only difference was that I had to tell them when to switch slides. It was a little bit clunky, but it worked. Eventually, we got video conferencing and I moved to conducting the orientations via that system. What I learned from this is that if it's important enough, you can make anything work.
>
> —Kathy

Is Orienting New Employees Your Job?

At this point, you might be thinking about how in your organization, the HR department performs new hire orientations. That's fine. It doesn't change the importance of what we've shared. If this is the case for you, it is still important to know what is being presented in the orientation and to ensure that you share any department-specific needs with HR and the new employee. This is particularly true if your organization is not 100 percent remote, and HR needs to address content that would not have been included in a generic orientation.

In other words, you should still work closely with your HR department to ensure a highly effective orientation process. In fact, you might suggest that orientations be split—one for proximity employees and a separate orientation for remote employees—so that each covers the necessary basics of the specific type employment. You could also ask to sit in on an orientation to get firsthand experience of the information being shared. Then, work with HR to tweak the orientation, if necessary, to include additional things you think would be helpful. Or, you might find that some things are easier to share with your new employees individually, and don't make sense to include in the formal orientation. Whichever works for you is fine. The point is simply to make sure the new employee has the most thorough foundation possible surrounding what is expected of them—and what they can expect from you.

Onboarding New Employees Is Your Job

As a manager, the onboarding process is a massive part of your role. Because onboarding is ongoing to aid in an employee's organizational establishment, it should include a variety of formal and micro trainings, check-ins, meetings, and opportunities to share feedback. Onboarding is a critical time to seek and test an employee's knowledge, skills, and behaviors. Every employee wants to become an effective, engaged member of their team or department, and onboarding provides the structure and guidance necessary to help socialize new hires within your organization. And honestly, it helps to shorten their time to proficiency, increases the likelihood of retention, deepens their engagement, and brings them closer to success and productivity.

But onboarding is more than just a random smattering of check-ins and experiences. Good onboarding is structured, containing multiple strategic, comprehensive, consistent, and measured stages and models of engagement lasting three, six, or more months.

A great starter onboarding checklist should contain some or all of the following engagements:

- a virtual welcome letter to the organization or team; you can either write it about your new hire or you could encourage them to create a video introduction of their own
- a virtual tour of your organizational technology, communications, meetings, and daily expectations
- assigned reading material for general training, orientation, and organizational insights
- an outline of your expectations as the new hire's virtual manager
- an introduction to organizational culture
- a virtual lunch with you, their manager (on video)
- an outline of their earliest expectations for the following week or month
- weekly or daily check-in meetings
- time to talk about short and long-term goals
- encouragement to connect deeper with the team or organization (such as through virtual happy hours, digital meet-ups, and so on).

The Predicament of Paperwork

Handling as much paperwork as you can electronically is awesome for a whole host of reasons—it can be easily and quickly sent, it takes up zero real space, and it kills fewer trees. But if a situation requires physical paper, you will need to cover it during the onboarding process.

Signed forms (think I-9s, W-4s, direct deposit forms, signed job descriptions, or employee acceptance forms) are important to have right at the get go. How will the employee get them to you? Can they be filled out online? Is there an electronic signature functionality so that the employee does not have to print out a physical piece of paper to sign? If that is not possible, does the employee have access to a scanner so they can print, sign, scan, and email the paperwork back to you? And if this is how the information gets back to you, how will you ensure it's secure?

It is not improbable that the situation will arise when sending forms electronically is not an option. What do you do then? Is the employee close enough to the main office that they can drop them off? Are they close enough that you can meet for coffee and a hand off? If they have to mail them, who pays for the postage? Is it expected that they will? Will they be reimbursed? There are lots of things to consider, but don't let this be a hindrance. Once your process is set, it's smooth sailing from there on out!

A Word (or Two) on Employee Handbooks

Over the course of this book it will become pretty clear that we are huge proponents of policies and procedures. They are the backbone, the very foundation, of a well-run, legally sound business operation. We know we're not telling you anything you don't already know. But to beat this dead horse a little longer, it's important that every employee understands the ins and outs of their employment, and the very best way to do this is to provide an employee handbook that is up to date at all times. This is another area in which you might want to work with your HR department to ensure everything is covered, and possibly even create a separate virtual employment handbook that includes additional policies and procedures that are unique to remote workers.

Furthermore, the handbook should be reviewed periodically—a good recommendation is to review it at least once a year—to make sure everything is current. If and when changes need to be made, it's imperative that every employee receive the amendment or update to the handbook—and sign off that they received it. We always want to be sure to "CYA" as they say—cover your assets!

A Few More Thoughts

✓ **Keep track of questions when orienting and onboarding.** Sometimes a new employee hits the ground running and doesn't have any questions; other times they're asking questions that you or your company has never thought about addressing but might want to consider. Jot these questions down and figure out how to answer them. It's very likely all new employees will appreciate the answer, even if they don't think to ask the question.

✓ **Note other topics to share.** Keep a running tab on any virtual topics and issues that aren't reflected in your orientation and onboarding experience but should at least be considered.

✓ **True onboarding is not reflected in a simple timeline or outline.** Employees will continue to have or seek answers to questions and will want to grow their own experience and expertise on the job. An onboarding process that lasts for six to eight months, compared with a few initial weeks, is the best way to ensure a new employee feels fully engaged and enveloped.

Signing Off

Have you ever played that game where someone has to describe how to draw something, without telling you what that something is? Inevitably this game ends up with a crazy image and some hearty belly laughs—instead of a tree, your picture ends up looking like a distorted stick figure that just stubbed its toe. This is where a poorly designed or delivered orientation could potentially lead—messy, muddled, disorganized chaos (but none of the belly laughs) that could have been avoided with a little thoughtful pre-planning and a partner mentality.

In this chapter, we've made the case that orientation and onboarding is an imperative component of the employee's experience. This is a time for you to set expectations for them. But remember, they have expectations too. Your new hires don't know what they don't know, so they are relying on you to paint as complete a picture as possible for them to describe what this remote position looks like in your eyes. Again, they *want* to do a good job and they *want* to please their boss. Your job is to effectively communicate what that looks like. If you can pull this together successfully, you've just struck employment gold!

8.

Day to Day

Managing a virtual team can get a bad rap. While being a virtual employee often invites conversations about wearing pajamas to work and playing on social media, managing virtual employees can have people thinking you're monitoring your team like some kind of Big Brother experiment or sending email after email of work duties and reply-all follow-up requests.

And if you're reading this thinking, "Um . . . I do monitor my team like a Bond villain and I do send dozens of emails every day about work and follow-up work," well then, sorry, we've got some good and bad news for you. The good news is that there are great ways to manage the virtual day-to-day workplace. But the bad news is you're doing it wrong.

Let's Level Set, Shall We?

Initially, many virtual managers fluctuate between two modes of management: overbearing and absent. Those who are overbearing think they need to be on top of their employees at all times—checking their instant messenger (IM) status, emailing or texting several times a day to check in or follow-up on things, or video chatting randomly to see how an employee's day is going. On the other hand, those who are absent managers assume that the tech will manage everything. They don't show themselves virtually for days (or maybe longer), respond only to emails that require a true follow-up, avoid video, and are never available on IM.

And sure, depending on your employees or your own manager, either virtual management style has its benefits. But when working in the virtual workplace, the topic of day-to-day management is not just about striking a balance, but creating an effective culture of virtual management. This chapter aims to tackle the true aspects of virtual management communications, involvement, and visibility.

Set Weekly or Daily Check-Ins

As any manager of any kind of workplace will tell you, you'll find that you check in with your employees for a number of reasons. In a stationary workplace, popping by an employee's office or cubicle can be as effortless as walking past on your way to use the restroom or to see if there are any bagels left in the break room.

However, these impromptu visits aren't as easy in the virtual workplace. So, we suggest a creating standing daily or weekly check-ins with your virtual employees.

The trick with a weekly or daily check-in is simple: Try to keep it at the same time, the same day, using the same format (call or video), and with a general purpose or agenda. We'd also suggest you make it brief by design. For example, a daily check-in could be less than 10 minutes or a weekly call could be around 30 minutes. If you need more time, you can always schedule for it. Keeping it short naturally means you'll focus on what matters—whether it's just to talk about the weekend or to drill down around a project. Then you won't feel like you have to fill up a full hour just because it's what you scheduled.

> *The first place I worked completely virtually was a small global consultancy where everyone was virtual. A favorite check-in model at the company was, at first, one of the weirder things I had to get used to: an all-staff daily check-in.*
>
> *Now, we only had 11 staff members so it wasn't too crazy, but the idea of having a daily virtual all-staff was so strange. However, what hooked me was the model they used, how effortless it was, and how extremely connected it made me feel. We would all get on the phone at 1 p.m. EST and go around on camera highlighting the one or two biggest tasks we were tackling that day. Then we'd go back around in reverse order to see if anyone had any direct questions the whole group might benefit from about anyone's specific tasks. If we thought our question was more one-on-one oriented it was tackled offline.*
>
> *These meetings usually lasted five to eight minutes and they helped us all feel more connected and like we were being seen and heard by everyone involved.*
>
> —Ben

Allow Good Tech to Aid You

In the day-to-day of it all, let your technology work for you as a manager. If your organization's technology offers shared access to your co-workers', employees', or team's calendar, use that to your advantage to grasp their role and goals for the week. Ask to be CC'd or BCC'd on emails that matter for updates or context. Use IM more often than email to get something tackled more quickly, rather than in a formalized way like in an email or during a meeting. Use video for check-in calls so you can see your employees and communicate more openly and earnestly, reading body language and creating deeper connections through sight.

However, don't think technology is supposed to fully manage autonomously. Be present! Use the phone instead of sending an email if you think the message would be better supported or supplied by a more personal or nuanced touch. Send IMs and respond to IMs received. And again, use video when you need to create a more appropriately casual working environment.

> *I have been working remotely in some capacity for the last 15 years. I quickly learned that having detailed written policies and procedures was going to be an essential component in the success of my remote working relationships. I like having a two- or four-week trial period for any new people I add to my remote team. These first two to four weeks are at a slightly reduced rate because I have found that while people say they know the various software you use to run your business effectively, they may really have no clue. However, I am patient through the learning curve if they can pick up new skills quickly. You also need to have contingencies for how the work will be completed on time if someone is ill for an extended period of time and how compensation will or will not be affected. Basically, you need to have backup plans for your backup plans. The joys of working remotely!*
>
> —Tracy V. Allen, TVA Consulting, LLC

A Few More Thoughts

✓ **Don't fall prey to stereotypes.** In a virtual workplace, some people wrongly think that virtual employees are more lax, lazy, or disconnected. Don't use your day-to-day management to perpetuate the idea that you believe that too. Don't use checking in to evaluate someone's workflow. Don't hide behind your own anxieties of not being able to see an employee's every waking move and assume they're not working or not working hard enough. Don't be that manager. Build a plan, develop culture, and manage humans like a human.

✓ **Exercise active listening skills.** It's extremely important for your staff to feel heard and understood. When you have your scheduled check ins, make sure to give each person a chance to express what's going on for them and create a comfortable atmosphere for them to ask for assistance if they need it. When they share, repeat back to them what you heard and ask clarifying questions to ensure you are both on the same page. Then do what you can to assist them. Win-win!

Signing Off

Nothing is easy. There are certain benefits to virtual employment, just as there are certain benefits to stationary employment. However, neither option should include managing the day-to-day details of your employees—no one likes to be micromanaged. Is it easier to pull someone randomly into your office while they're walking by to check in? Maybe for you, but what does that feel like for your employees? The same can be said for the virtual employees—is it easy to just randomly call them or reach out on video? In many cases, yes, it really, truly is. But again, who is that easy for? For you. How does it make your employees feel?

The truth is that it doesn't matter what kind of employees you manage—stationary or virtual—the value of day-to-day management is in the management part of the equation. It's about crafting a plan, creating a culture, and not over- or under-extending your reach as a manager. It's about making it effective for both parties for purposeful reasons. Not just watching from some virtual ivory tower or hiding under the wires and dull plastic exteriors, but being a present manager with a role, a purpose, and a smart approach.

> *Overall, management in my case wasn't top shelf when I was an on-site employee. I shouldn't have expected a more collegial relationship when I became a virtual team member. In fact, deadlines became more arbitrary, and communication became less frequent and more opaque. When I asked for clarification, or guidance, or just about anything, I got comments that invariably included phrases like "you're at home, so can't you make the time?" A 25 to 30 hour a week position became nearly 50 hours a week, but no commensurate increase in pay.*
>
> —Karen Johnson, Principal, Stopgap Freelance Service

9.

Meetings

Meetings. We all love them or hate them. Well, mostly hate them. And while the virtual workplace is many things, it's not exempt from the need and importance—and sometimes drudgery—of meetings. So the least we can do is offer some best-in-show solutions for how to tackle meetings in the virtual workplace. It's something that takes a little more planning and tact than you might have realized, but will set you on the path to make the best out of a situation we often happily villainize.

Let's Level Set, Shall We?

In the virtual workplace you have a variety of mediums to leverage for hosting and conducting meetings. From IM to social media platforms, conference lines to video conferencing, there are a variety of ways to approach meetings in the 21st century, and not all of them are suitable for your needs and purpose depending on the circumstances.

Instant Message

Assuming your group isn't too large and you're not trying to deliver a ton of nuanced or heavy information, you can host meetings on an instant message platform. IM is a great way to host a brief meeting to tackle short, simple tasks, such as what to eat for lunch or where to meet for a working session. You can also use IM to quickly get initial impressions from co-workers or employees about a candidate after an interview session or following the release of some breaking organizational news.

Our point is that it's a meeting forum that works for pithy, quick, small meetings.

Social Media Platforms

There are a wealth of platforms that allow groups to gather online in threads or group chats to host meetings or discussions; Slack, Yammer, and Jive are just a few of these messenger-styled platforms. These platforms allow for meetings where everyone's input needs to be captured more cleanly and in order, but also allows people to link articles, photos, documents, and more for other users or storage. You can also use these platforms to facilitate virtual collaboration for meetings and more, assuming everyone has access.

Conference Calls

The conference call is the classic "virtual" standby. The granddaddy, so to speak. But it's also the one that gets the most flack and is made fun of the most. Not every conference call system is built the same, and things like dropped calls, overlapping muting, and not being able to see who is and isn't on the call can make this platform frustrating. Having said that, the conference call is still a strong platform for hosting meetings of all kinds no matter the size or purpose. It's still—in many ways—the perfect meeting equalizer because people are often most comfortable with this medium, which allows them to fully participate with ease. And while not always ideal, also allows for some level of multitasking when appropriate.

> I worked with a professional membership group of international doctors; their work was virtual by default because they were located all over the world. One of my responsibilities was planning their mid-year in-person meeting, which was one of only two opportunities they had each year to be physically together. However, one year there just wasn't money in the budget or time in the doctors' schedules to meet in person, so the president decided to hold the meeting via video conference. We took two consecutive Mondays for four hours at a time and held our mid-year meeting on camera.
>
> This was such a fantastic way to accomplish what they needed to, save money, and still experience the next best thing to actually sitting next to one another. Even breaks were fun. Everyone would take the time they needed to get up and stretch or use the restroom, but then grab a snack or a drink, come back to their cameras and socialize with each other for a few minutes before getting back to business.
>
> —Kathy

Video Conferencing

If conference calls are the granddaddy, video conferencing is the smart, but rowdy teenager—confident in its own abilities, but in such a way that it makes everyone else feel awkward and slightly unconfident. That being said, video conferencing is the bridge between the stationary and virtual workplace. And as Ben (weirdly) likes to say, "If you say you miss stationary workplaces but you won't go on video, then I guess you're just awkwardly saying you miss the way people smell?"

But all jokes aside, video is a great medium for just about any meeting type, size, group, need, purpose, and goal. The advancements in this medium have come in leaps and bounds. Today, not only can dozens of people be on camera at once, but you also have the ability to digitally share documents, have off-camera texting and conversations, pose questions, take polls, and much more.

> There's a lot that can be missing in communication without being in person and we've found that it is important to recognize that and check in with folks to ensure we are understanding one another and are all clear in ways that are either more explicit or more frequent than we might if everyone was in person. Part of this means defaulting to video all the time. Staff are very rarely on the phone with other staff; instead, we are on video conferences (Google Hangouts, for example). Building a culture where the immediate response to a potential conversation is to get on video with one another helps remote staff feel more included, and supports better communication because everyone can see one another's faces.
>
> —Amy Sample Ward, CEO, NTEN

A Few More Thoughts

Beyond picking the right medium for your meeting, we want to make sure you have a wealth of other solid tips, tricks, and ideas for running a successful virtual meeting. You may already know some of them, but they're all worth mentioning:

✓ **Have an agenda.** People want to know what meetings are about and why, what role they might play, and why they're invited. This fact doesn't change for virtual audiences.

✓ **Respect everyone's time.** Time is money and time is precious. Virtual or not, start meetings on time and end them on time. This is another fact that's not virtual-specific but universal in nature.

✓ **Solicit ideas and insights from all involved.** Unless the meeting is top-down—and then it could be an email or perhaps more like a training session—it's important to provide opportunities for people to contribute.

✓ **Send supporting documents in advance.** Depending on your meeting medium, sending documents in the middle of a meeting or expecting folks to read things—or worse, being read to during a meeting—is a waste of valuable time. Sending documents early if possible is smart so people can familiarize themselves with everything, helping the meeting run more quickly and smoothly.

✓ **Test equipment or conferencing platforms in advance.** Mistakes happen, failures happen. But if you simply don't know how to use the platforms or are unsure of how to manage them well, you'll do more than ruin the meeting, you'll likely tarnish your reputation in the virtual workplace.

✓ **Don't forget introductions.** If some of your employees are not on camera or if it is a voice-only conference call meeting, make sure everyone announces themselves so all are clear on who is in "the room" and how to best proceed.

✓ **Press record.** Recording meetings in the virtual world is a wonderful thing. It gives you the opportunity to send the recorded meeting to participants later instead of sending notes or in addition to notes. It also helps the notetaker because they can stay more engaged during the meeting and refer back to the recording for more details if necessary.

✓ **Take it offline—online.** When something can be addressed in smaller groups or handled in different meetings or more one-on-one, run your meetings in a way where those situations are recognized and the rest of the meeting can continue to take place.

Signing Off

Meetings get a bad rap, but it's because they're often just seen as groups of people getting together to talk. Nothing more, nothing less. Virtual meetings can be the absolute worst if there is no plan of action, bad management, and the wrong virtual medium. You need to make sure that your virtual medium is being employed correctly and matches the purpose or size of the meeting. If you really need to "meet," think smartly about how, where, when, and why. And we promise that while you'll never singlehandedly make meetings cool or valued, you'll at least make sure *your* meetings aren't despised.

10.

Communications, Awkward Moments, and Casual Screw-Ups

We've all received an email or text message where the tone didn't come across as intended. Were they being rude or ironic? Or were they simply trying to make a joke? Or maybe they were just being blunt or tone deaf or sarcastic. Sometimes it's really hard to tell.

It's times like these you realize that a winky-face could really make or break the message. Then again, emojis could make it worse. Why did they send a crying face? Did they mean the laughing crying face? Why a cow? How do I interpret a cow emoji? A tomato? What on earth?

Now, imagine how these scenarios play out on a day-to-day basis when working in the virtual world. What happens when you're working virtually and you or those you manage make a serious mistake? What if you send the wrong file or refer to a client in an email by a competitor's company's name? Or, what if you hit reply all on an email chain where you or someone else said something inappropriate or snarky about someone in that "all" category? We've all been there. Trust us.

Let's Level Set, Shall We?

When an awkward or seemingly tragic situation happens in an office setting, you can rush to the cubicle of the hurt or confused person, ready to apologize, cupcakes in hand. Or you can quickly run to IT to see if the reply-all can be reversed before anyone has a chance to open the email. Or heck, you can even attempt an *Ocean's 8*–level heist, asking the person you might have offended to join you for coffee cake in the break-room while your best friend/co-worker sneaks into their office to delete the email directly off their computer. (Inspired imagination? True story? *We'll never tell.*)

The simple truth is that awkward moments and screw-ups happen. And as a virtual manager, you can help avoid some of the most casual issues.

Discuss Your Communications Standards

Everyone has a different way of communicating. Some people are thoughtful and methodical. Others are fast talkers. Some can't help but use humor. And others are dry and pithy.

With a million other styles to consider, how this plays out in the virtual workplace can get complicated. This is especially true since most communications occur in writing or over the phone. And even when they take place on camera, they're not the same as an in-person conversation because many people feel awkward when they know they're being filmed. One of the very best things you can do as a virtual manager is talk to your employees openly about your organization's communication style.

In a nonprofit that I worked for, we had a mixture of both in-office and remote work. Being such a small office with limited staff and much work that needed to be done, it was extremely important for staff to get the uninterrupted time they needed to complete work on various projects.

We implemented a system whereby we used the status buttons within our email platform to indicate whether or not we were available at the moment. We could add an emoji (like a stop sign) and a short description of what we were doing (such as "phone call," "meeting," or "working on website") to indicate that we should not be interrupted during that time.

This became invaluable to us both in and out of the office. When working remotely, we also used it to indicate when we were at lunch or away from our computers. This simple communication method was also shown to new employees during their orientation, setting the standard for how we worked and what the expectation was.

—Kathy

Some workplaces are extremely casual—co-workers and supervisors may send an IM with meeting minutes in one message and a funny meme or gif in the next. However, others are far more buttoned up. Some require the use of formal memo systems or track IM or email usage to gauge personal versus professional intent. Keep your staff informed of which type of workplace you are in.

When mistakes are made and awkwardness happens, laying out the basis of your organization's internal communications style helps your employees understand how to begin rebounding from errors. Keep an open door policy and check in with those who report to you on how their virtual interoffice and interpersonal communications are going.

Being Unintentionally Rude or Inappropriate

One person's humor can quickly be read as inappropriate. And one person's directness can quickly be read as rudeness. When the wrong intention is assumed or acknowledged in the virtual office, there isn't a magical solution. Much like in the physical space, you just need to:

- Apologize.
- Explain yourself (if appropriate).
- Ask if you both can move past the incident.
- Truly move past the incident.

Awkwardness, like they say about misery, loves company. And that company? More awkwardness, usually. Once you can get past it, just get past it. Don't keep apologizing. Don't attempt to turn it into a joke. Don't make it your middle name. Apologize, explain, move on.

As a manager, it's also just as important to learn from the situation. You may not have realized you hired a former class clown until you watch them shoot for laughter on every conference call. Or you struggle to get a new hire to speak without being called upon. Use these moments to create an open dialogue on the topic. Schedule 15 minutes to talk about it openly and constructively with your employee. And invite those you manage to do the same with you when necessary. Nope, it's not always fun, but trust us, neither is ignoring it.

Sending a Mistake in an Email, Document, or Resource

As a virtual manager, your job is to help your employees succeed, which means it's on you to train your people and remind them that professional mistakes aren't cute. But mistakes in communications happen. And you'd be hard pressed to find someone who's never experienced it on the sending or receiving end.

So, how you can handle communication mistakes in a virtual world? First and foremost, remember that the world is driven less by what happens than how we choose to react to it. Take a deep breath, don't panic, and then put a plan in place to help you and your employees deal with any damage:

1. **Hit pause.** These things happen. The worst thing you can do is go into full-blown apology or repair mode before you have complete grasp of the situation at hand.

2. **Fully assess the details of the mistake.** Was it one email or document to one person or a large batch email or document to a ton of people? Did you catch it early enough to avert any damage? How big was the mistake and what was its impact? There can be a big difference between getting someone's name wrong or getting a date or process step wrong.

3. **Plan your response.** Once you've assessed the situation and its impact, you can begin to do something about it. We've all been that person who forgot to attach a document, apologized seconds later for not sending the attachment (but still forgot the attachment), and finally attached the document to the third email in a chain of painful apologies. Don't make that mistake! Figure out the damage, be quick to respond, clearly address the mistake and correction, apologize, and move on.

4. **Pay attention to the impact details.** Assuming you've accomplished step 3 with success, it is in your best interest to track every outcome of the situation. The larger the error or audience, the more likely what you did in step 3 didn't work for everyone. So, is any

follow-up necessary or are there questions you still need to answer? Do you need to issue any form of correction or apology, such as on social media or by a message from a higher-up in the organization? This won't be fun, but it's often necessary when mistakes are made.

5. **Learn from your mistakes.** Did you think your proofreading skills were pretty good before you sent that email with a massive typo? We bet they get even better after you make a mistake. Or perhaps you need to ask your direct reports to send you (or a communications or editorial team) their materials for a few weeks so you can review them and help make sure there are no more mistakes. No matter what happened, there is something to learn and something to gain. And yes, sometimes there is something to lose—like a job— but we'll tackle that in another chapter.

Getting Information Wrong or Being Unclear and Running With It Anyway

We've all gotten a confusing email from a co-worker or boss. Not the kind of confusing where they start writing in Klingon in the middle of a sentence, but the kind where they write with vague directions, maybe with the occasional emoji, suggesting you have prior knowledge that would put their message in context. But you don't. Or at least you don't remember.

In a virtual world, it's no less awkward than it is in person to take the extra second and ask for clarity or a reminder. But you should do it anyway. And make sure your employees do the same. A culture that doesn't make time for clarity or level-setting is prone to making any number of mistakes over time. The old carpenter proverb of "measure twice, cut once" is true in most professional and virtual settings.

Admittedly, this isn't easy to train for in advance. When things happen—and they will—it's important to address them as part of the continued dialogue so everyone can work through and learn from them. If you don't, they can lead to misunderstandings or confusion, or, worse, to unintentional rumors and gossip.

One time I got a business IM from a friendly co-worker that read: "Jason is coming home today 😂."

Getting random, casual IMs at this organization was very culturally normal. And at first, I wasn't even sure why this co-worker was messaging me. Looking back I should have responded with "Hey, how are you? What's going on?" or something that helped me help her realize that either the message wasn't meant for me or that I wasn't sure what she was talking about. But I remembered that she had a college-age son named Jason. And because I didn't want to look foolish or out of sorts—and because I didn't know she had used the crying-laughing emoji by mistake—I simply wrote back: "Yeah, sometimes when your kids come home after being away for so long it makes you want to run and hide or lock all the doors, am I right?"

Unfortunately, what I didn't remember was that Jason had joined the military. I also didn't know that he had recently been killed in active duty. And I certainly didn't know "coming home" meant that his body arriving back in the U.S. for her to pick up. To this day, I shudder when anyone sends a slightly cryptic message with a crying-laughing emoji; however, the error was on me for pretending to understand something I truly knew I didn't and responding blindly anyway.

—Ben

A Few More Thoughts

✓ **Being put on a project with a team or co-worker who isn't as focused as you are.** As a manager, you need to level-set on team contributions and how the work does or does not get spread equally. Do it on a conference call or via video chat, because not discussing it openly can lead to a free-for-all, and that's never good for anyone. Ideally you would have this conversation on the front end of the project when everyone explains how they see their role and how much time they have to devote to the role. In the middle of a project? That's OK! Open it up for discussion now. Go over roles and timelines and responsibilities like adults. Because you are adults.

✓ **Right or wrong—correcting or disagreeing with a superior or subject matter expert in a group setting.** Ah, the cut that stings both ways: disagreeing with a superior. This is sort of the king of all awkward workplace moments when it's not received or handled well. In some settings, it's appropriate to disagree with a superior and express as much. However, correcting a superior can be complicated. There's a difference between having a dissenting opinion versus flat out telling someone they're incorrect, wrong, or backward, and the latter is not the ideal way to address the topic. Instead, get them on camera or the phone to address the topic and make any necessary edits. In an in-person meeting in a stationary workplace, you can usually read the person's body language, allowing you to react and reroute. On the phone or in a video chat, it's a different story. So, unless you feel confident in how you and your superiors typically interact when you disagree, discuss that issue as a sidebar.

✓ **Dealing with someone who wants to chat more than work.**
We've all been there: a co-worker or supervisor pops into our IM, sends an email, or calls or video chats just to vent or talk about their weekend. It can be nice—at first. But then it drags into the rest of the morning. Then a long IM convo in the afternoon. And then another chunk of your evening. Only after the fact do you realize they've taken up a sizeable portion of your day with blather and chit-chat. Now and again? Fine—we all need days like this. But when it becomes the norm you need to address this behavior as a manager. If it's happening to you, you might consider not responding. (This works as a suggestion for your employees too.) If the person asks "Why didn't you respond to my text/GIF/funny story!?" You can say, "Oh, sorry, I've just been really busy, and didn't have a chance to respond." It's true, it's simple, and it's the best way to keep someone at bay in the right way.

Signing Off

Awkward is as awkward does, as one might say. The trick is to plan ahead when you can, and be prepared to address things openly, honestly, and transparently when they happen. Never lose sight of the best ways to approach a virtual world when awkward things happen or mistakes take place. More than ever this is the worst time to shoot off an email condemning or attempting to correct a problem. Text messages are even worse. The best option is to schedule a call or jump on the phone or video chat. Humans make mistakes; don't double down on them by making more and attempting to tackle their repairs like a robot.

11.

Performance Reviews and Promotions

Performance reviews. We all have a love/hate relationship with them. Just doing *one* takes so much time, thought, and effort that the idea of doing one for every member of your staff can feel pretty daunting. As a manager you may have handled tons of performance reviews already. Or maybe you haven't. Either way, performance reviews are an essential part of how virtual employees are often seen, motivated, and evaluated.

This is one of the opportunities you, as a manager, have to invest in each individual employee to let them know how appreciated and valued they are. You get the chance to build your virtual team up by recognizing them for the amazing work they've done over the last year (or however long it's been since the last review), while also having an open and honest conversation about areas that need improvement.

The time you spend focusing on each staff member is a

high-mileage activity that can take your organization to the next level. Who doesn't want to be noticed and praised for the work they've accomplished? We'd even dare to suggest that staff are also appreciative of your constructive feedback because everyone wants continued growth.

Your employees should have the opportunity to have their hard work and dedication formally recognized in their personnel file. Now, we bet the question you're asking yourself is, "Is there anything different about performance measures for a virtual employee?" The short answer is yes. There aren't a ton of differences, but there are enough that it matters. Make sure you know the details to make your virtual management the best it can be.

Let's Level Set, Shall We?

We've already talked about the importance of the hiring process and making sure you have the most trustworthy and capable people on your team. Once they are on your team, they need a very clear, very specific set of performance measures to work toward. Why? Because people want and need to feel like they are being productive and doing meaningful work—and that is no different in the virtual environment. They want feedback beyond the daily or weekly communication you're already having.

The Importance of Virtual Performance Measures

In the chapter on hiring and interviews we talked about thinking through the entire process before you begin. This includes whatever performance measures you want to have in place. If you are hiring for an existing virtual role you can simply review the current performance measures, but if it's for a brand-new role, you will have to think through what these measures look like for that position.

We recommend setting up a merit-based system from the start—one where you know if someone is doing a good job based on the quality of their work, as well as their ability to meet deadlines. This might take a little more up-front effort on your part, but it will provide another layer of evidence when making decisions about promotions. Additionally, set clear guidelines for promotions. Don't make your employees wonder if or when a promotion will happen. Outline a clear hierarchy to work toward—if you want to see your staff work hard, give them clear goals.

Think about it. When you cannot see your employee on a minute-by-minute basis because they are working around the world or completely different hours from you, performance measures are the absolute best way you have as a manager to determine how your employees are performing. And that in turn is the best way to know that your virtual employee is working out—they know what work they have to do, they know what their deadlines are, and they get things done. This is also a great way to build trust and rapport with your virtual staff; they know that you trust them enough to point them in the right direction and watch them go.

What Makes Reviews Different for Virtual Employees?

Performance reviews, we believe, have changed over the years. They're no longer just a litany of what an employee did right or wrong or a one-sided monologue that focuses more on the manager and the organization than the employee—or at least they shouldn't be! Today, performance reviews should spark good, productive conversations between the employer or manager and the employee. And in a virtual employment setting, performance reviews become even more important elements of an employee's work experience.

Checking in periodically with a performance review that acknowledges goals the employee has met (or even crushed!) and identifies the areas in which more action is needed or new goals that need to be set is crucial for the employee's development and career path. This type of review also benefits the organization because an employee who feels recognized and appreciated is more likely to go above and beyond for their employer in the future.

The other obvious difference for performance reviews with a virtual employee is the fact that you may not be physically together when it's time for the review. If it's possible for you to meet in person (for example, you have budgeted for travel or live close enough to easily get together), that would be great. The next best thing is video conferencing. Doing a performance review over the phone can be acceptable, but only if no other way is possible.

Why use video? Because it's important for you to be able to see each other's facial expressions and body language. Video also lets you see and feel empathy and understanding coming from the other person, which will help to make the performance review as effective as possible.

When scheduling the time and location for the performance review, you and your employee should find places that are free from distractions and interruptions because you'll be discussing private and confidential information. Also, make sure that you give the review the time it deserves, and that neither of you have to rush off in the middle of it to another meeting or call. Remember—this is one of the most important conversations you can have with your staff, so treat it as such. Also, be sure to log on a few minutes early so you can test the tech, make sure the sound and video work, and so forth. Once the review begins, you want to be able to stay on track and focus on the conversation at hand.

Beyond Reviewing Performance

In addition to their daily work, you're also supervising a variety of additional workplace details and expectations for virtual employees. You can use performance reviews to talk about these things too. Ask how they're doing with new or existing workplace technologies and tools. How are they doing in their home office? Are they working well with or relating to others in the virtual workplace? There are many topics about the virtual workplace you can cover that are probably not included in the metrics and outline of a traditional performance review.

This is your opportunity to really drill down and offer insights, support, or just an empathetic ear about performance and attributes unique to the virtual workplace. Don't forget that.

A Few More Thoughts

✓ **Don't host the review from a coffee shop.** Meetings like performance reviews are personal, professional, and private in nature. So, make sure you're in a secure space and that your employee is too. If they work in an environment where a spouse or family member is nearby or could be within earshot? Ask them to move to a more secluded place in their home.

✓ **Make note of cultural relevance.** In a virtual workplace, culture is key. So don't lose sight, during performance reviews and promotions, of how employees are or could be struggling to adapt to the culture at your organization. This could include issues such as not feeling comfortable speaking on conference calls, adjusting to different time zones, or even discomfort with "letting people into their home" on video calls. These are often organizational culture issues that need to be learned, not just understood, and can make the difference between an employee who is struggling or truly thriving in the workplace. Your job as a manager is to make them easier or more transparent when you can.

Signing Off

Performance reviews should never be negotiable or only happen "if I get around to them." They should be done on a consistent basis, whatever that looks like to you. Trust us, employees desire that interaction and look forward to your feedback. Since virtual staff aren't with you every day, they truly feel valued and are more likely to thrive when you dedicate time with them to set goals, evaluate their contributions, and highlight their accomplishments.

12.

Professional and Educational Team Development

In the world of virtual management, out of sight should *never* mean out of mind. Even if you never meet in person, you are still managing real people, and they deserve to be treated as such. A good manager, whether stationary or virtual, recognizes the need for educational and professional growth, and then provides those opportunities to their employees. They understand that it is an excellent and necessary way to ensure growth for their organization as well as maintain and even boost the morale of their staff.

When it comes to educational growth in the virtual setting, while many options are similar to those for employees in a stationary setting, you can be sure of one thing: they're almost always going to be experienced virtually or online. Despite the proliferation of e-learning programs, many people are accustomed to doing professional development in a conference room or small break-out room. Further, even if your organization offers e-learning programs, they still require people to look at their screens or be on camera or attend another—different—conference call. So e-learning can often feel like "more of the same." We believe the key to virtual educational growth is ensuring that educational experiences feel important and purposeful. And that takes more than just offering a typical virtual experience.

Let's Level Set, Shall We?

People want to feel important enough to be invested in by the people around them. In an employment setting there are many ways to invest in your people, but we believe that offering educational opportunities is one of the best. It also gives you the most return on your investment. People want to grow and learn and not stagnate. So, when the opportunity for professional growth is offered to employees, it's as if their manager is saying, "I believe in you and I value your work in our organization. I want to see you learn and grow both for the benefit of the organization, as well as your own personal edification."

That would feel pretty darn good, wouldn't it?

We also suggest that you create professional development plans with each of your staff members. This is an excellent opportunity for you to demonstrate the value of your staff by asking them to find courses or conferences they think would be helpful and send you a list of the courses and the costs associated. Work together to develop a plan that makes sense and both of you can be excited about. This is wonderful way to demonstrate your investment in them. Look at the skill areas required for each position and then determine how those skills can be honed or increased. Then find educational opportunities that serve each area. Set goals for each employee to reach and continue to set new ones as they accomplish those goals. Build in time to each employee's weekly or monthly schedule for educational opportunities. And make sure you solicit feedback and suggestions for improvement from your employees about the professional growth program. If you have regular all-staff conference calls, ask everyone to give an update on their educational progress, maybe sharing one or two things that they plan to implement in their position.

Education in (and for) the Workplace

Learning and education is so important that people actually look for continued education offerings as a perk when they are job seeking. We've all heard that saying, "what if I train them and they leave?" But we would argue that if you invest in your employees, they will invest in you, which then feeds into an employment relationship that becomes a mutually beneficial one. Doesn't that sound amazing?

Growth is important for all employees—and that doesn't change for virtual staff. In some ways, educational opportunities are one of the few "tangible" benefits a virtual employee has, since they are not able to enjoy the free soda and cheese balls in the physical office (though we do have ideas on this, which we cover in another chapter). Continued education is something that can really cement the working relationship. It shows your staff that you believe in them and you want to invest in them as much as you expect them to invest in you. Virtual employees can also struggle to land promotions or raises in recognition of their hard work, so offering them developmental opportunities can help make their career advancement more accessible.

Many employers have line items specifically for professional growth in their budgets. Check to see if your organization does too. If it doesn't, we encourage you to speak to the powers that be to see if it's something that can be added to future budgets. It really is that significant.

Digital Bliss

Online education—which can be anything from free webinars to postgraduate degrees—is the easiest way to provide educational growth to your virtual employees. Many colleges and universities offer online programs, certificates, and degrees. And attending an online training program can be much less expensive than an in-person college or university.

Webinars

When it comes to online webinars, allow your staff to participate in webinars they think would be beneficial to their position. While some webinars cost money, others are free. Do staff need to get prior authorization to register for a paid webinar? One option would be to create a policy allowing staff to take any relevant webinar without prior authorization, as long as doesn't cost more than $25. Of course, this would only make sense if you had a line item in your budget for education.

Additionally, if you see a webinar you think would be a good fit for someone on your team, pass it along! Just make sure they know exactly why you forwarded it to them, whether the webinar is optional, or if you have decided it is mandatory.

Certifications

There are online certifications for countless different specialties today. Online certifications are more expensive than webinars, sometimes costing a couple thousand dollars, but they could prove very valuable to your organization. We suggest making sure the certification is specific to the position and would allow the employee to level up in their performance.

Group Education and Training

Another great way to educate your staff is through group training. Hosting webinars or online working sessions are easy ways to offer virtual trainings to your employees. Consider bringing in a guest speaker to talk about trends in your industry. Another option is a group coaching session. Do you oversee a department that has two or more people? Could you hire a coach to work with this department and develop their skills? This could be a cost-efficient way to provide valuable education to your entire team.

Higher Education

A coveted professional development opportunity is the ability to take courses at a fully accredited college or university. This can be a huge draw for virtual and local employees alike, if your organization has the budget and ability to support it. Sure, it will take time to earn a degree, but the new skills employees implement along the road to completion can really take your organization to new heights.

Note that it is perfectly acceptable to stipulate (in writing, of course) that an employee has to remain with the organization for a certain number of months or years after completing their degree to secure the return on your investment. If they leave, they would then be responsible for paying back the money the organization spent on their tuition.

A close second to this option is offering tuition reimbursement. In this case, the employee could take courses from the college or university of their choice, based on whatever parameters you set. Then the organization would reimburse the tuition after it has been paid. The fine print is different for every organization, but you may include stipulations that an employee has to achieve a certain grade or maintain a specific GPA before the reimbursement is processed.

A Few More Thoughts

✓ **Invite educational development as a topic of conversation.** It's OK for an employee to ask you about their professional development. But if you want to be a better manager, don't make them ask. Take the initiative and start the conversation.

✓ **Share relevant, work-specific content.** As a manager, you could send a Friday email digest sharing some of your favorite blogs, reports, or articles from the week. And don't just share work-related content; include wellness or self-care pieces to show your employees that you care about all facets of their role and their person—inside and out.

✓ **Really strapped for cash?** If you don't have the budget to pay for online courses or degrees, at least keep the educational ball rolling by encouraging your staff to read books, listen to relevant podcasts, or take the free or low-cost webinars for the time being. But keep the lines of communication open and let your employees know if opportunities for deeper, more fulfilling educational growth arise. You may also want to spend some time seeking grants or major donors that could invest in your team's professional development.

Signing Off

Allowing staff to spend time and money on educational growth is one of the best things you can do for them. Education is something people carry with them their entire life—it's something that cannot be taken away. But as we all know, education can be expensive. That's why it's important to create a line item in your budget to cover education. Plan for it—education shouldn't be an afterthought.

And, dear manager, don't forget to include yourself when creating professional education plans! If you take this aspect of employment seriously and act on it, you will see returns on your investment that reach far beyond you or your employee being more knowledgeable.

Finally, we would encourage you to remember that different people learn in different ways, so don't assume that the same method will work for all. Some people are readers, some need to see it, and some need to do something to learn it well. Keep this in mind when developing your professional education programs.

13.

Bandwidth

Bandwidth indicates the amount or capacity that something can handle at any one time. Unfortunately, as technology gets faster and faster and increasingly mobile, we've unintentionally started to tether the bandwidth of technology to the bandwidth of people. Sorry folks! These are two totally separate things.

Let's Level Set, Shall We?

Within the 24 hours of every day, there is only so much any one person can accomplish. Some tasks are quick and easy; others require much more time, thought, and effort. Also, what takes one person a few minutes to do can take another quite a bit longer (we're all unique individuals!).

And then there's a little thing called priority. If something needs to be done immediately or simply can't be rescheduled, we often have to make it work and get the job done. Unfortunately, our normal work does not stop flowing in like a mighty, raging river, and it can be hard to remember how to tread water, let alone swim.

So, if we start each day with the same 24 hours, what does that look like in terms of bandwidth? This chapter presents a few tips to keep your company running like a well-oiled machine without making employees feel like they're just cogs.

Protect the Environment

When it comes to bandwidth and (potentially unintentionally) encroaching on someone's limits, you need to consider your environment. Your work environment, that is (although your work environment might include a few plants, so who are we to suggest they don't overlap?).

Is your work environment open and inviting enough that an employee would be comfortable approaching you if they felt like they were reaching max capacity? Have you created a welcoming space that encourages openness and communication? Have you communicated that to your staff? Even a virtual workplace can have an "open door policy" if handled correctly.

It is much easier to be proactive and intentional about creating an open and communicative work environment. You want your people to come talk to you as soon as they're feeling stressed, rather than trying to push through and burning out because they reached max capacity long ago but were too scared to talk to you about it. Of course, this is a two-way street—if someone is naturally shy or finds it difficult to speak their mind they still need to be willing to tell you if they're overwhelmed. Otherwise, they really have no one to blame but themselves.

No matter who you manage, it's still your job to manage them and the environment you occupy. You may need to make a point to communicate openly with your employees in addition to simply creating space for them to communicate openly with you. Consider asking how their bandwidth is during your weekly check-in meetings; don't just ask how it is within their current workload, but also on a broader scale. Consider asking what one thing they would take off their plate if given the opportunity, and use their answer to gain some insight into how they are balancing their work. You should also consider asking them how technology can offer more support in the virtual workplace; or perhaps it's one of the reasons they need more support in the first place.

Be Realistic With Your Expectations

As a supervisor, it is not your responsibility to know how to do every single task your staff performs. But you do need to understand how much time is required for your staff to do their jobs well and efficiently. If you do know how to do a task, imagine yourself doing it. If you don't know all the ins and outs of a task, ask an employee to keep track of the time they spend on it. How much time does that task realistically take to complete? Is it actually possible for one person to complete everything included in their job description? Is there a better way to distribute all of the work? Is there a way that makes more sense? There are lots of things to think about, but this is all part of achieving—or maintaining—that managerial "rock star" status!

In fact, many tech collaboration and communication platforms have the ability to track the amount of time spent on a project, if you turn those features on. It's important to recognize that implementing a time tracking process may spark some initial anxiety among your employees. And yes, if implemented incorrectly, the tracking might make them feel like Big Brother is trying to squeeze every digital second or penny out of them. That's why transparency and open communication is so important! If you're open about the purpose and intent—you want to help them use their time wisely and avoid burnout—time tracking can be a fantastic tool in your virtual toolkit.

The real message here is that you should always be communicating with your staff about what they're doing and then evaluating how it's affecting their workload. This also means that you may have to occasionally adjust job descriptions and shuffle tasks to create a better balance. Be open to this. Sometimes adjustments need to be made and that's OK. This is all part and parcel of creating the best possible work environment. Keep the lines of communication open with your staff (see the communication chapter for more advice). You'll thank us later!

The Elephant in the Room

OK, we can't move away from this topic without talking about the bandwidth elephant in the room: What are the parameters for working remotely? In a proximity position, it's very easy to see when a person is working—they arrive at the building, they work at their desk, and then they leave the building when they are finished. But just because your remote staff doesn't physically come in to a brick-and-mortar office building every day doesn't mean that they don't have to follow "regular" work hours. And while the majority of their work is done online, that doesn't mean they don't also get work done when they're offline.

Working remotely does not equate to working constantly. And your staff should not feel as though they have to be available around the clock to remain in good standing. This is another area in which you need to manage your own expectations as a manager. How much *you* work is up to you—you may be a workaholic who doesn't mind working 15 hours a day or on the weekend. But we urge you not to project your definition of work hours onto your staff. Set expectations with them—and then remember (and respect!) the expectations that you set.

Be Ready, Willing, and Able to Change

No program, department, plan, or project is perfect. They can always use improvement—and that's a good thing! We can only grow if we are open to change and willing to make the adjustments necessary to advance our cause. So, if an employee tells you that they are overwhelmed with their workload—in general or even just during an unusually busy time—hear them out. Investigate the situation. Ask questions and be open to making necessary changes to ensure the smooth operation of your department.

Take a minute to consider what responsibilities or projects might be shifted or eliminated altogether. Could technology play an increased or decreased role? We've seen it happen many times—an organization has great ideas for new things to implement (projects, programs, and so on), but fails to realize that something else might need to give. Or that learning new things not only takes time, but can temporarily create new problems in the present, even if they'll eventually solve problems in the future. You cannot keep giving your people additional work without taking away some old, tired things to make room for the new things to be learned and take root. Simply piling on new tasks will put you on the express lane to employee unhappiness and probably cause valuable team members to leave.

To be very clear, we are not saying that you should go into complete upheaval mode every time someone feels a little extra busy. Busy seasons happen, and sometimes everyone just needs to suck it up and soldier through. You also need to keep in mind that some people are pretty quick to over-glorify the idea of being busy. We also hate the thought of burdening other staff members with more work because of one squeaky wheel. You need to understand and accept that sometimes things *are* imbalanced. As the manager, it is your job to see it and then determine how to return balance to your department.

A Few More Thoughts

✓ **Solicit feedback from your staff on a regular basis.** That starts with creating an open and welcoming environment for communication. Make sure that regular communication with your employees is a priority. Ask leading questions on a regular basis to make sure you're always touching on issues related to bandwidth.

✓ **Investigate and be willing to change where necessary.** Understand what is required of the positions that fall under your authority. But also give your staff the opportunity to work out imbalances between themselves—this will help them feel empowered.

✓ **Don't take advantage of your staff.** Your employees work to live, not live to work! Don't assume that working remotely means they're working constantly. Avoid sending staff text messages "after hours," unless it is a true emergency.

✓ **Manage your own expectations.** When *you* work is up to you. Set communication standards with your staff and stick to them like they mean something. Because they do.

Signing Off

Everybody has a limit. Everyone has a certain bandwidth that they work within—and it's different for everyone. As a manager, you need to find the balance between "Sorry, this is what the job requires" and "Sure, let's figure out what can be changed." You can't classify every cry of maximum bandwidth as DEFCON 1; you also can't ignore every cry for help on the basis of "the job is the job is the job."

Know your people. Understand them and their positions. This will be your best and most productive approach to ensuring that your staff and the work you are all responsible for completing are as balanced as possible. Remember that just as technology slows down as we reach its bandwidth limits, so too do people. In that way, the two are similar.

14.

Disciplinary Meetings

Nobody likes to talk about (or to be the recipient of) disciplinary action, but sometimes people do things that make it necessary to address those things in a way that is fair and equitable for all.

You want to believe when you hire a new person that you've hired the *right* person. When making your decision, you trust your gut and your intuition and most of the time, that works out just fine. Other times, it doesn't. But whether it's a brand new employee or the employee who has been with you the longest, "offenses" can happen. Sometimes they're big and very clearly against policy. Other times they're more subtle, gray, and maybe even somewhat . . . understandable.

Whatever the reason, and however much you won't want to, you'll need to have that disciplinary meeting. Even virtually.

As we've discussed in other parts of this book, our aim is less to give you a bunch of best practices within your organization's policies and procedures, and more to give you the tools, ideas, and suggestions for how to make disciplinary meetings work effectively in a virtual setting. That said? We do want to share a few best practices as to how to conduct an effective disciplinary meeting.

Let's Level Set, Shall We?

Hopefully your policies are clear on what is acceptable behavior in your virtual environment and what is not, but it's mission impossible to cover every single scenario in an employee handbook—so don't even try. But let's agree to something right here at the beginning: Any and all disciplinary action that needs to be taken should be perceived as an opportunity to review your policies and procedures and make adjustments when necessary. What gaps need to be filled? Are some of your policies unclear? Where are they perhaps *too* strict? And where are they not strict enough?

Ready. Set. Let's Make a Plan.

Like anything worth doing—even if it's not a fun thing to do—you should start with a plan. But this isn't just any meeting. This is a serious meeting about the behavior or actions of someone you supervise, and trust us when we suggest that it's fine to acknowledge that it might be unpleasant for both parties. What you need is a solid disciplinary action meeting plan, or DAMP.

A good DAMP isn't that complicated and most organizations have one you can follow. But in case yours doesn't, here's a simple eight-step DAMP you can use right away, or use as the base to start creating your own:

1. Get all the files in order. Make sure you have the employee's file and any formal details or documentation of the disciplinary issue.

2. Prepare for the employee discussion. Create the outline, build the questions, plan for the follow-up, consider inviting a third party, and so forth.
3. Schedule the meeting.
4. Conduct the meeting.
5. Review the agenda and stick to it.
6. Ask for input or create space for input to be provided.
7. Provide a copy of the whole thing.
8. Schedule a follow-up meeting.

You are an adult, so we're not going to break down each step—most of them are pretty self-explanatory. But we do want to take a closer look at a few steps for the sake of supporting your efforts as a virtual manager.

Step 2: Inviting a Third Party

Disciplinary meetings can be awkward, and sometimes you need to have an additional person present. We encourage you to reach out to your HR or legal team to determine this decision, but we also want to address how this can work virtually. You'll need to use a service that offers more than just a one-to-one video meeting. These days almost all video conferencing services offer multi-participation features; if yours doesn't, consider using a free or third-party platform that ensures all who are invited to the disciplinary meeting can and will be able to effectively attend.

Step 3: Schedule the Meeting

Have you ever been pulled into a meeting where you were yelled at or told you had done something wrong, with no warning or time to prepare? It's never fun to be blindsided. It's not the ideal way to deal with a disciplinary issue in the virtual space either. Not just because it's an ineffective way to deal with these kinds of meetings, but also because you need to be on camera.

Even if a virtual employee spends a large chunk of their day on camera, it's still not commonplace to just video call anyone, anytime. Is it acceptable? Sure. But while these meetings should be done swiftly, you should still schedule them. If this isn't possible, give the person at least the slimmest acknowledgement of notice so they can tidy up their desk and straighten their dress shirt or pajamas. We're not here to judge.

More important, and just to make sure we're being crystal clear: Don't perform a DAMP over the phone. Or email. Or smoke signal, while we have your attention. If there was ever a time when video is necessary, it's when you as a manager need to deliver difficult, critical, or essential news. This is not the time to pretend video isn't the next best thing to "being there."

Step 4: Conduct the Meeting

Conducting a disciplinary meeting in a virtual setting isn't all that different from a stationary one. With that said, let's talk about how to conduct yourself on camera.

Author Jordan Wellin (2017) said it best in his WISTIA article, "The Science Behind Why Your Gestures Look So Awkward On Video":

> Our movements and posture are things we feel, but rarely see ourselves doing. Our posture reflects how we feel and conveys many nonverbal signals. So when you see yourself looking confused or flustered . . . it's important to remember that the way you feel in your body and the way you feel in your head are linked [on camera].

The point here is that you might want to think about being a little more reserved in this meeting. A little more stoic. A little more relaxed, but in a calming and professional way. Because what you don't want the person on the other end of the camera to see your angry eyebrows, flailing hands, and frowny faces—not only will they read these cues as you being non-verbally aggressive, but you will likely be thrown off by it as you watch yourself in the tiny box in the corner of the screen. This is a serious meeting, and your body language needs to be taken just as seriously as the words you choose.

But be real too. If your relationship with this person is typically laid back and relaxed, you don't want to take a posture or tone that is too buttoned up or robotic. You want to make sure that the person knows this is a serious matter, but in doing so, you don't want your own behavior to come off as completely unnatural. It's a fine line, we know. But somebody's gotta walk it!

Step 8: Schedule a Follow-Up Meeting

This is an essential part of any DAMP, the follow-up meeting. Assuming the person isn't being fired, it's important to create space for a return to the topic to see if there are any further thoughts, actions, or discussions that need to take place. (And if they are being fired, check out the next chapter, which is all about dismissals.) Please don't think it's acceptable to just roll a follow-up into your next one-on-one meeting. This should be a brief follow-up that is mutually scheduled to close the loop or make sure the loop can be closed around the subject.

A Few More Thoughts

✓ **Don't record the video.** Unless you have been given express permission from your HR or legal team, recording your conversation is not an option. Don't even toy with the idea; there is no good reason and it only serves to unnecessarily escalate the circumstances. Also, in some states, including

California, it is illegal to record communication with employees unless they agree, usually in writing.

✓ **Don't conduct this meeting in an open office or public setting.** You should avoid public spaces for this call. When you schedule the meeting make sure to suggest that the person you're talking to finds a private space to take the call if they typically work in a public or nonprivate space, considering the subject matter.

✓ **During the meeting, don't make accusations.** Present the facts as you know them and as they're outlined in the DAMP. Explain *why* something is unacceptable if they don't understand.

✓ **Use the phrase, "Explain to me why. . . ."** This will help you get their perspective. Don't make them feel defensive or embarrassed.

✓ **Treat the person with dignity and respect.** Talk *with* the person, not *at* them. Depending on what happened, they may have already beaten themselves up over it or they may be on the defensive, so treating them with reserve will help defuse the situation where possible. Alternately, they may not have a clue that they've done anything wrong, in which case they deserve the space to feel and react the way they're going to feel and react.

✓ **Remember the purpose of the review.** The goal is to come to a resolution—not to belittle or embarrass them. This is also why the follow-up meeting is so essential.

✓ **Ask questions.** What do they think is the best approach for moving forward? What changes do they think they can make to ensure the same thing doesn't happen again? Ask these questions again during the follow-up meeting.

✓ **Consider how to handle the rumor mill.** The potential for gossip is especially high when other members of the team know the meeting is taking place or know the details of the situation. Even in a virtual setting, the rumor mill is real and needs to be quelled or addressed if necessary.

Signing Off

In more ways than not, a virtual disciplinary meeting isn't that different from one done in proximity. However, this is a case where the little things count: Make sure the meeting is done on camera for best results, be mindful of how you might come across on camera, and ensure as much privacy and protection as possible for the call. These all translate to a proximity setting, but become even more essential once cameras are in play.

At the risk of sounding like a broken record, this is a human issue like any management situation, set to the tune of technology. Never forget that you're talking to a flesh and blood person with feelings and needs, and that you have a duty to address these issues with decisiveness and discretion. The technology just serves to make it happen seamlessly in a virtual world.

15.

Dismissal

Letting someone go from their position—just thinking about it can give even the most steeled, experienced managers the shivers. There is probably nothing that falls under a manager's purview that is more loathed than having to fire someone. It is not fun and it is never easy. But sometimes, there is no other choice and it has to be done. The real trick here is knowing how to handle it well in the virtual workplace.

Let's Level Set, Shall We?

You've had some issues with a certain employee. You've discussed these issues with them, documented everything, written them up when necessary, and yet, the problems persist. The decision has been made to let them go because keeping them would be detrimental to the organization. Now comes the hard part. How the heck do you handle a dismissal with a virtual employee?

A Virtual Goodbye

Much of the dismissal process will closely mirror the process in the stationary workplace. However, when dismissing a virtual employee, there are a few things you need to consider. First and foremost, you want to make sure you have everything documented and have consulted your HR department. Unfortunately, you never know if a dismissal will end up in an unemployment hearing, or worse, a legal case. You must make sure you have the right folks informed and all your facts are straight and at hand for such occurrences.

Once you have everything in order and it's time to have that difficult conversation, set up a time to talk. This is another time that we believe it is best to use video conferencing, but if that is not available to you, a regular phone call will have to do. Give your employee some advance notice, but not too much—maybe an hour or two. It is likely the employee already knows what is about to happen and—although we hate to think like this—you want to make sure the employee doesn't have time to do anything destructive such as delete files or create a cybersecurity threat.

Be sure to treat both the conversation and the person with respect. Remember, the employee may not be a terrible person; it may be just a series of unfortunate events that brought you to this place. Explain fully the reason for their dismissal, and be sure to cite any prior conversations or write ups that led you to this decision. This is their livelihood—they deserve to know fully and clearly what is happening and why. Exhibit empathy toward the person and give them some time to process and allow them to speak or ask questions. However, don't get caught up in their emotion when answering. Once they have said what they want to say, let them know that you will be following up with an email outlining all the details and the things you discussed. You will want to request their personal email address, because you will be deactivating their organizational email immediately.

Video vs. Phone

You likely wouldn't fire someone over the phone in a stationary workplace, and that same thread of reasoning is true in the virtual workplace too. So, while you might only have the phone at your disposal, we really want to stress that using video truly is the best way to have the dismissal conversation. Why? As a manager you're expected to manage any employee until the very last moment of their employment, and video allows you to not only hear how the employee is reacting and feeling, but also see it.

Also, in the same way you might invite someone from HR to an in-person firing, you might also want to consider inviting a superior or HR representative to join the video or call as well. It never hurts to treat firings the same no matter the kind of workplace; just make sure you have all your bases covered and that sometimes includes an extra guest on the technology.

CYA—Covering Your Assets

Many virtual organizations have the ability to turn off employee technology, untethering them from important files or email at the push of a button. This is something that you should consider for your processes.

If you've kept good records from the start, you will know exactly what company-owned equipment the employee has in their possession. It will be up to you to determine which items you want returned and which you don't. Perhaps your organization has an equipment policy stating that after three years the equipment, for example a printer, becomes the property of the employee. Technology changes so fast that it might not be worth paying to ship back a potentially antiquated piece of equipment that just sits around until you figure out how to dispose of it.

You will also need to arrange the payment and shipping methods—whether that means pre-printed UPS labels or reimbursing costs associated with shipping. You'll want to figure out as much in advance as possible, and then, as always, document everything. After the actual conversation takes place, send a formal dismissal letter via email (and perhaps certified mail as well) outlining all the dismissal details (for example, if severance is included, the employee's vacation payout amount, and date of final pay), as well as the parameters around equipment retrieval. You want to make sure that nothing remains unclear because it will be a very awkward conversation if that employee needs to call or email you to clarify a detail of their dismissal.

Another important thing to consider is what to do about any organizational credit cards or authorizations the employee has. You may want to deactivate the credit cards right before your call or immediately thereafter. It is never easy to lose a job, and, unfortunately, people can become angry or vengeful in the process; as a manager, make sure you think of everything the employee has or has access to before you make the call.

A Few More Thoughts

✓ **Have a checklist ready for returns.** Create a list of all the items a new hire receives or has access to, and have them initial that checklist as they receive each item. Then make sure to keep it up to date throughout their employment. That way, when they leave—whether on their own or because you let them go—it will be much easier to quickly see what they have, what they need to return, and what access you need to deactivate.

✓ **Maintain confidentiality.** Avoid the temptation to talk about the firing experience with your co-workers or team members. Of course it was difficult! Of course you want to vent. But respect the dismissed employee's privacy enough to keep this matter confidential. Besides, it's just the ethical and right thing to do.

✓ **Follow-up on follow through.** Think through all of the follow-up that needs to occur after the fact, such as sending the detailed follow-up email, deactivating anything that needs to be deactivated, figuring out how that person's tasks will be covered, deciding how to proceed with hiring the next person, and notifying stakeholders of the change.

✓ **Be mindful of your own self-care.** Firing someone can be extremely stressful for the person who actually has to do it. Make sure you take some time for yourself that night or that weekend to really decompress so you can release the stress and carry on as the best you can be.

Signing Off

If and when the day comes that you have to be the one to let someone go, you'll likely find it to be one of the most difficult days you experience in your working life. Try to keep in mind that, if it has come to this, it is the best decision for the organization. Keeping this at the forefront of your thoughts will make the process at least a little easier, because ultimately you want what is best for your organization and your team. Be respectful and kind, but also refrain from saying too much, because anything you say could later be brought up and used against you if any unemployment or legal claims come against you. Remember—what you don't say can never be misquoted or misinterpreted.

Most importantly, take time for you! This is tough stuff and you will need to find a way to release the experience, especially if you are a highly sensitive person. Don't deny yourself your need for self-care and the time you need to process.

16.

Family, Friends, and Nepotism

We've all seen it: A family business with multiple family members working together. A president or CEO who hires their teenager to do administrative work. A co-worker who passes along a job opportunity in your company to their best friend, who ends up getting the job. These situations can all turn out fine. More often, however, they end up being messy. So as a virtual manager we're tasking you with working hard to avoid this mess and identify what nepotism might look like in a virtual setting to ensure you're not contributing to the problem.

Let's Level Set, Shall We?

Nepotism is a fancy word with a simple meaning. It refers to anytime someone in a position of power or authority plays favorites or gives special privileges to someone that they know, be it a family member or friend. Although nepotism may be a little harder to detect in the virtual setting, the results of an employer "playing favorites" can be very much the same. We are not suggesting that family and friends should never be hired within the same organization. However, the way in which it is done, and the policies and procedures surrounding it, should be thoughtfully considered to avoid problems in the future.

Hiring Friends and Family: What Could Go Wrong?

Although we like to focus on the positive, there are some cases in which we need to discuss the potential downfalls of a particular area—and this is definitely one of them. When considering the morale of your team, having the right people working for you is of major importance. Having the wrong person—or even the right person in the wrong position—can wreak havoc on your team's morale. How? Well let's consider the boss whose wife is hired on and reports directly to him. Suddenly, the team starts to notice that the wife is receiving "special treatment" by way of a more flexible schedule so she can run home to get the kids off the bus or more lenient accident forgiveness when mistakes are made.

Other members of the team will easily pick up on these perks; in fact, most will hold the management of an employee's friends and family members under much stronger scrutiny. Smaller teams, in particular, tend to have their fingers directly on the pulse of what is happening in the organization at any given time—it's hard not to! They say that perception is reality, and what is perceived as nepotism can turn into something that resembles an invasive plant that keeps growing until nothing else in the garden can be found. And who wants that?

I worked for a small virtual organization that had several family members working with one another. The founders were family and in the early years it was easy to bring family and friends into the fold to keep costs down and because they were trusted and loved. But as an outsider, it was strange to work on a vulnerable project with the sister-in-law of the founder. When they disagreed with each other, often making it personal, I had to unpack not only the problems with the project, but the pots and pans of their lives too. And because it was virtual, I couldn't always just look them both in the eyes and tell them to knock it off, like I might in a stationary environment. I had to sift through more of their chaos than I would have liked to, until we found common ground.

—Ben

How to Avoid Unnecessary Problems

Here are some general guidelines when dealing with nepotism in the virtual workplace. Whether the employee is proximity or virtual, the spouse (or any other relation) should *not* be allowed to report directly to the person they're married to; they should have a different, unbiased and objective supervisor. Second, they should not be given special treatment to take care of things like getting the kids off of the bus, simply because of their relationship with the boss. It's OK to have a flexible, understanding, and lenient environment for your employees if that's what you choose (see the chapter on flexible schedules for more on this topic). But back it up with policies and very clear expectations, then extend it to *all* employees, not just the ones with relational privilege. Also, when mistakes are made, the same disciplinary procedures should apply to all employees.

Virtual settings present additional challenges when working with family or friends. Does the boss's spouse get special or better equipment to work with? Does one cover for the other to get an extended lunch period, or to skip work altogether because of something going on in their family life? It's not fun to think about these kinds of things happening, but unfortunately they do. If two virtual employees in the company reside in the same household, extra care should be taken to clearly explain what is expected of them—whether one of them is the boss or not.

It's up to you as a manager or the other "powers that be" to create a work environment that is devoid of nepotism. This is not an impossible task, but it is one that takes thoughtful advance consideration, backed up by clear policies and procedures. Even if your work environment is already virtual, it is absolutely worth being proactive by reviewing the policies and procedures that exist, and thinking through any additional ones that would be helpful. It is always better to tackle things proactively than to be forced to respond reactively to a situation that has already occurred, which also creates the added stress of having to figure out what to do on the spot.

Ultimately, you want to be able—and should be able—to trust your staff. And most of the time, especially if you have good hiring practices, you are able to do so. But it is always better, and easier, to be able to fall back on a policy or procedure that is already in place about issues such as favoritism or nepotism than to have to make things up as you go along.

A Few More Thoughts

✓ **Address nepotism when hiring.** Adding even the simplest mention of nepotism as a no-no in your hiring or application guidelines can save you and your organization a lot of headaches.

✓ **Alert HR.** In cases where you see problems with nepotism, it's not a bad idea to inform HR. You don't need them to immediately intervene—unless it's necessary—but you can at least suggest that you're having to address actual or potential issues now for something that might become more complicated later.

✓ **Never lose your professional edge.** While issues related to nepotism often feel extremely unprofessional, that doesn't give you license to handle them unprofessionally. Make sure you are covering all topic areas of concern directly and appropriately, especially in the virtual workplace. Don't send texts or private messages expressing your general frustration. Handle this like any other grievance or issue worth managing.

Signing Off

Nepotism can be really ugly and it can destroy the morale and productivity of your team. If you have a friend or family member working at the organization it can be easy for you to do little things for each other that may seem like nothing. We don't think that anyone practicing nepotism does so intentionally. But what seems like nothing to you may seem like a very big deal to other employees. Ask yourself how you would feel if you saw others doing the same behavior. Would you think it was unfair? Would it make you uncomfortable? Let's remain mindful and keep things fair and transparent.

17.

Snow Days, Elections, and Holidays

It's rare for the power to go out completely in a stationary workplace. When it does, sometimes a manager has a plan for making sure the day's work still gets done. Other times, and we've been there, no one has a plan, and everyone just sits around in the dark for half a day waiting for their lights and computers to come back on so they can get to work.

An organized workplace should have predetermined procedures for snow days, holidays, and special events like championship parades or major road work. Likewise, there's a need to plan for these events in the virtual workplace—what do you do when the lights go out, the Wi-Fi is down, or delays are caused by upgrades and updates?

Let's Level Set, Shall We?

While a big part of the format and expectations for "unusual days" are usually outlined and determined by HR, the virtual manager needs to deal with some things no matter the policy or procedure. These are the topics we want to cover in this chapter.

Snow Days, Elections, and Holidays

Virtual managers manage people everywhere, anywhere. One person's winter is another person's mudslide season is another person's monsoon season—and the list goes on. At the end of the day, anyone can experience a terrible weather day that might result in having to keep the kids at home, losing power, or dealing with household or community damage. What's a manager to do when these problems occur and there is no formal policy?

Determine Communication Flow

Depending on the circumstances, your virtual employees might not be able to access their work technology to even let you know they're not able to work. Do they have your phone number to text or is it easy enough to call you on a landline or email you on their phone? (Do they know how to send smoke signals? Can you read them?) No matter the details, it's good to let your employees know how to reach you when problems arise.

Help Your Employee Express Their Needs

You don't need a full grasp of their problem to understand their needs. It's not your job to play reporter during times of strife. Whether the problems are big or small, if your employee needs to take time off or reschedule their work, or if they simply (and temporarily) cannot work, we encourage you to meet them where they're at and work on a solution to the one thing you can control: their workload and work schedule.

Set Expectations on Checking In

Assuming they're not just taking a few hours off or coming back the next day, make sure to ask your employee to check in each day using your determined communication flow plan.

Sometimes the Problem Is the Tech

Broken upgrades, tech flaws, update problems, and more can limit or prohibit your virtual employees from completely engaging in their job. Make sure as a virtual manager you're not just aware of these problems, but that you're helping your employees or the team responsible for solving the problems stay on top of the solutions. It's never fun to be without the necessary tech, but it's even worse when you have to deal with it all by yourself.

> One time at a major organization I worked for, we were switching email systems and I was one of a small handful of remote employees with no functional email because of some system failures. During that time, I had IT run a proxy against one of my personal email addresses so I could at least keep getting email, but I couldn't send emails to anyone but a small handful of co-workers who wouldn't be confused by sending something to my work email but having me respond from my personal email. It wasn't perfect, but it at least solved half my problems for a few days.
>
> —Ben

A Few More Thoughts

✓ **Consider what to do on Election Day.** More and more employers are giving employees the entire day or the necessary time off to vote or volunteer during national, local, and special elections. Just like any other day, this is a great topic to cover with your policy and leadership teams, but also something to consider independently as a manager, if you're able and you think it would add value for your virtual employees.

✓ **Respect unique holidays and life events.** As we covered in the chapter on diversity, inclusion, and equity, make sure virtual employees have the ability to celebrate and experience holidays and special life events that matter to them. As always, plan ahead! Give them the insights and time necessary to make plans while acknowledging how the work will get done (or placed on hold) while they're out. Also, be sure to keep your international staff in mind. Their election days, holidays, and even acts of nature could be completely different. Keep those lines of communication open so you always know the unique needs they have when it comes to these things.

Signing Off

Virtual managers need to know that all management is essentially change management in the virtual workplace. You should not only anticipate and prepare for change; you should welcome it, forecasting and strategizing within the knowns and unknowns to ensure your employees believe they're being treated fairly during times of need or frustration. Thriving managers in a virtual workplace never see this as falling under the "other duties as assigned" banner, but instead embrace this reality as part of their managerial responsibilities.

You may think it's the job of IT to handle technology upgrades or that the individual employee needs to figure out what to do if they lose Internet access at home. And maybe, given your policies, that's true. But unless it's written down somewhere, it becomes your job as a manager to forecast likely possibilities and respond to needs or outline the expectations for when they happen. Because they will happen. Snow will fall. Houses will flood. And diabetic cats do need to check their insulin every two weeks at the vet. Yes, that last part is very specific. Don't ask.

CULTURE IS KING

Understanding and Building Virtual Teams

18.

Team Building

We get it. Mentioning "team building" in a workplace setting can elicit many—drastically different—reactions:

Nooooooo!
Oh, cool!
Are you $%&# kidding me?

That's because most teams employ familiar tactics, which the more extroverted members love and the lesser so ones hate. But when they work well, team building activities are an important part of the workplace, helping to develop team dynamics and morale. There are countless books, blogs, and websites out there that can give you a wealth of ideas and team building techniques to use.

Team building is important. These activities can create powerful relationship dynamics, allowing your team to bond. By learning about one another's strengths, weaknesses, interests, and expressions, your team form the building blocks of better communication and fuel a stronger ability to grow and thrive in meetings or on group projects. And as a form of extracurricular, these activities can be a nice change of pace—room to breathe and opportunities to engage in some constructive awkwardness. Team building exercises let people feel like they're in the safety of a laboratory where they can try new things, and even if a few things spill over or blow up it's all part of the plan, not a mistake or fallout.

Here's the rub: How do you translate team building effectively for the virtual workplace? In this chapter we'll open our bag of tricks to reveal a few virtual-exclusive team building activities you might not find elsewhere.

Let's Level Set, Shall We?

Let's get one thing clear: Team building in a stationary environment *is* easier. There. We said it. It's truly easier. And 75 percent of most team building activities are basically exclusively designed for people who are all physically present in the same room. Think about it: The Human Knot? The Marshmallow Challenge? The Egg Drop? The Office Olympics? These classic activities are fueled by being able to see and touch your teammates. They're basically impossible to carry off in the virtual workplace without some heavy virtualization or editing.

But don't worry. This is less about being "creative" or "inventive" and more about truly understanding the *power* of team building and how that effectively translates over email, text, messenger, phone, or video. Because, yes, when it comes to team building, you should use all the classic virtual office tools at your disposal. That makes it far more fun.

In Team Building, All Tech Is Good Tech

Some forms of workplace technology are better than others, depending on your needs, but when it comes to team building, more technology is better than less. By this we mean that leveraging multiple forms of office technologies is a great way to make the activities feel more "physical" to those in the virtual setting. Get creative!

So, does this mean you should have a fax-off event? Hmm. You know what? *Maybe.*

To help paint a picture of how to use something other than a fax machine, we're going to share several virtually dynamic team building activities you can use at your next team building or employee engagement event. Some are virtual riffs on old standbys and others are more unique. Enjoy!

Virtual Scavenger Hunt

Easy, simple, and fun. A virtual workplace scavenger hunt can take so many forms: It can be educational, where everyone is learning while playing; it can be constructive, where the hidden objects build to something bigger; or it can be a generic, simple, fast-paced activity in which groups collect or gather a certain number of things just for fun.

Keep it variable. Don't just have teams search for things around their house or office (such as cling wrap, a stapler, throw pillows), but also have them find things online (for example, a link to a YouTube video, a cut and paste of song lyrics, a screenshot of the geolocation map of your favorite hot dog shop).

You can also add variety through the vehicles for proof— stipulate that one task has to be sent to the whole team via email. Another could be that you have to text the next person searching on your team before they can start looking. Make another something you have to show to everyone playing on camera. This makes it a little more frantic, but a whole lot more fun.

Coco Chanel Challenge

Coco Chanel famously said, "Before you leave the house, look in the mirror and take at least one thing off." She may have been talking about bracelets and baubles, but this is a fun idea to apply to simple office tasks. For example, have people pair off and write each other emails, except instead of using their hands, they can only use their elbows. Or have everyone on camera, but facing away from the camera, try to fold a paper airplane while their partner explains how to do it; then compare notes. Essentially, do something normal, but take one thing "off" to make it more interesting, virtually.

Endless Possibilities

Ask everyone to share a random object from their home or office (they can show it on camera or take a picture and text, IM, or email it). Then ask everyone else on the team to guess what the object is and how it's used. This activity works best when everyone shows something that is unique, odd, or difficult to figure out, because it frees the other participants to come up with wild and creative answers. It's also a fun way to get a virtual "look" into each person's home and life without making them vulnerable or feeling too pushy.

A Few More Thoughts

✓ **Determine your purpose before you plan.** Why are you doing team building? To build morale? To offer some ice breaking opportunities? To "get away" from your desks for a bit? To help your team grow and gel? No matter the reason, there are any number of team building activities that work virtually to meet your needs. You just need to do a little research and map out how they'll accomplish the goals you want to achieve for your team.

✓ **Consider creating a team building planning committee.** Just because you're a manager doesn't mean you have to come up with all the bright ideas alone. Create a small virtual committee (a pre–team building team) with other people who love the idea of running smart and simple online activities. This is a great management tool, but an even better place to exercise delegation and democracy skills.

✓ **Give introverts room to breathe.** One of the biggest complaints about stationary workplace team building activities is that introverts suffer under the pressure and stimulation of all the talking, touching, and madness. In a virtual team building event, you can significantly limit those elements by making activities less about talking and more about doing tasks, like the Virtual Scavenger Hunt, or performing activities over email or text, rather than having to be on camera or the phone.

Signing Off

By now we hope we've convinced you that team building is not terrible—terrible team building is terrible. And if you don't have a plan to bring these exercises to a virtual playing field, you risk them becoming pretty terrible and falling flat. So don't just have fun with virtual team building, get smart too. Use the entire platform of your workplace technology. Get others involved early. And determine your purpose before you start, so you can avoid blindly searching for activities, and focus on ones that will work for your team and your goals.

Oh, and lose the whistle. Anyone who thinks it's cool to bring a whistle to a workplace team building event—stationary or virtual—is a horrible person. We stand by that truth.

19.

Maintaining Morale

Maintaining good morale in any workplace setting can be a bit of a challenge, so it's important as a virtual manager to do what you can to create an environment where morale is high, but also recognize when it's not—and then do something about it. And frankly, doing both is equally important. We understand that sometimes there is nothing you can do to stop morale from decreasing, but if you keep your finger on the pulse of your team's morale you can act immediately when you see it starting to decline to keep it from going further. Don't be like the orchestra on the *Titanic*—continuing to play as if nothing was happening around them, despite the fact that the ship was literally sinking. We're sure the fish were impressed, but the guests still suffered.

Let's Level Set, Shall We?

Morale can be a very abstract concept to try to wrap your head around. It's not always easy to define, but it's typically fairly easy to gauge, especially by your employees. They know when things are not right as they interact with their co-workers and discuss how they feel about the current temperature of the organization. In a stationary workplace, low morale can be difficult to see until it's a problem. But in a virtual setting it can be more than difficult—it can go undetected until it's palpable and destructive. So you need to keep your radar up and your morale-building skills intact and ready to go!

Work hard, play hard was a frequent mantra of mine leading a consulting practice with more than 90 percent virtual employees, including myself. So, if we were planning a practice or department meeting, I would incorporate a theme to enhance the experience regardless of whether the individuals worked at headquarters, another office, or from home.

I still remember one department meeting after a multi-team restructure, during which we were discussing ways the teams would need to work together to implement the new solutions on the horizon. It was during the 2016 election season, so it felt fitting to incorporate a debate theme. The twist was that each team could only debate "views" (products) that other teams would normally deliver. We scheduled the debate for the end of the meeting, appointing managers as "moderators" and asking each team to nominate their "candidate."

The activity not only encouraged the teams to learn about each other, but it was apparent many also had fun with the theme. One candidate even created a podium in his home office, which everyone could see via Skype! True political views were off limits during the meeting, ensuring everyone could have fun learning about other products.

—Jena Blaustein, Nonprofit Business Management, Senior Consultant, Blackbaud, Inc.

Virtual Morale

In your virtual setting, there are four different levels of morale you need to recognize and respond to. Each one requires you to be constantly proactive in your approach. Those areas are:

- creating good morale
- maintaining good morale
- noticing and triaging sinking morale
- rebuilding bad morale.

Good morale begins with happy employees. Happy employees are those who are treated well and fairly; have meaningful work to do; work with a team that they know has their back (and doesn't talk behind it); and have a manager whom they can trust and is easy to approach no matter the situation. Some of these will be out of your control, but most are not.

Creating Good Morale

Creating good morale starts at the very beginning during the initial hiring process. Do your best to conduct conversations with prospective employees using video conferencing so the person can see your facial expressions and body language. Then be sure to portray your enthusiasm for the organization and communicate the best parts about being employed there. This will excite them and make them want to be a part of your team. Even if this isn't the candidate you ultimately end up hiring, you've at least raised some positive awareness about your organization. And if it *is* the person you hire, continue to create a good foundation for virtual morale by offering a thorough online orientation and onboarding process (see our chapter on this for ideas). Make sure you also express your open-cyber-door policy—they should know that you're available to them whenever they need you (for anything work-related, of course). Establish this positive relationship right from the get-go and you've laid the foundations for good morale.

But what if you're managing an existing team? How do you create good morale within a team you inherited? Great questions! In this situation, you want to make sure that you either create or continue to build on the strong, sturdy foundation of open dialogue, constructive conversations, goal setting, and helpful performance reviews with each employee. We talk about each of these in other chapters of the book. Ultimately, just follow the golden rule—treat others the way you want to be treated.

Maintaining Good Morale

Once you release your new employees into the cyber realm, it is a little more difficult to maintain the fuzzy feelings they got during the hiring and onboarding processes, especially after the novelty of a new job wears off. But it is certainly not impossible. There are a few things you can do in the virtual world to help maintain good morale. For instance, hold weekly or bi-weekly staff meetings (on camera preferably) to check in with one another. Make these meetings upbeat and fun. Even if something somewhat negative comes up, direct the conversation to focus on the positive aspects of it, or at least some positive steps you can all take toward rectifying it. You want your team to leave these meetings feeling like they were heard and that they have actually accomplished something. One of the fastest ways to kill morale is by having pointless meetings. (See our chapter on meetings for more.)

Another tip might be to have one-on-one chats with your team members every few days to ask how things are going and if you can be of assistance in any way. Put reminders on your calendar so you don't forget to have these chats. What can seem very spontaneous to the employee can actually be something very intentional for you—and that's OK. They don't need to know that. Employees who feel cared about and who feel like their manager is on top of things and knows and understands what is going on in the organization are happy employees indeed.

In our chapter on educational growth opportunities, we speak about the importance of incorporating education into your virtual team's benefits. Did you know it's an excellent way to maintain morale too? Especially if education is offered, as opposed to something they have to request with fear and trepidation. If you are investing in your employees in this way, it helps them feel valued and respected, which are two important pillars of good morale.

One last tip in this category is to celebrate the team's accomplishments and milestones—both personal and professional. We have a chapter on this, as well, with a plethora of ideas, so check it out! When you acknowledge someone for a thing they have accomplished, it makes them feel good. Morale is all about feeling good. So make them feel good!

Noticing and Triaging Sinking Morale

Sometimes moral slips. It happens. No need to feel guilty; management is hard and morale can slip for a number of reasons. Maybe it's just an extra busy time for your organization and your staff are feeling the pressure. This makes the gauge on the morale-o-meter start to tick down a bit, but you likely just need to ride out the season and morale will improve on its own. Other times, there are things you can try to keep morale from sinking lower.

If you're asking yourself how diminishing morale might show its ugly head in a virtual workplace, you are asking exactly the right question! While low morale often shows up in exactly the same way it would in a stationary workplace setting, it may be a little more difficult to identify. Morale might be low for one single employee, for example, which could present itself as an act of insubordination. If you can catch it and address it with that one person before it spreads, that's awesome! Remember, the hallmark indicators of good morale are cheerfulness, confidence, and productivity—it's how your employees feel about the organization, and certainly one employee can have negative feelings about the workplace.

But low morale is like an invasive plant that spreads rapidly throughout the ranks. So quickly, in fact, that by the time you start to see the symptoms, it's already set in. This is even more true in the virtual setting. So how do you recognize it? Perhaps you notice an increase in gossip—if the ole grapevine seems active, it's a good bet there's something going on. Or perhaps it's a sudden decline in meeting participation. If you notice that several or more people are not interacting with the group or offering ideas or suggestions in your team meetings, this could be a good sign that morale is low. Other indicators include a general lack of care and enthusiasm, increased call-offs, or, worse, turnover.

So be vigilant! During these times it's important to notice low morale, catch it, and stop it in its tracks. Even in a virtual world, you should make every effort to recognize when someone or several someones aren't acting right. Trust your gut and investigate the details. It is perfectly acceptable to have a meeting and ask your staff to explain their perceptions and feelings. Tell them you've noticed that things seem a little off and then ask if something is going on that you can help with. As a manager, always treat your team as partners and be there to serve. As always, it's important to hold these meetings on video conference. Your team needs to see your concern and willingness to help. This will lend itself quite nicely to building or rebuilding good morale. If you've created an open and approachable environment, they will likely not have any trouble answering your questions.

Rebuilding Bad Morale

What happens when something big goes down and your team's morale is shot? Or what if you've been handed a team whose morale tanked right before you took over? Either way, it's a bad situation that's never beyond repair. This is when you to swoop in and do what you do best—you build, you create, you talk, and you invite others in.

Your efforts at rebuilding bad morale can benefit from many of the tips we shared about creating good morale, because you truly are starting from the beginning. Actually, you're often starting from below zero in these situations. And that's not always a bad thing. Starting from the bottom means the only way to go is up and forward. Clearly there is rebuilding that needs to be done—and you, confident virtual manager, are just the one to do it. We encourage you to set up individual phone or video calls with each member of your team to really get to the root of the morale issue. Ask them questions such as:

- What do you think is and is not working within our organization?
- How do you think the situation can be improved?
- At what point did you start feeling this way?
- Was there a single event or circumstance that caused your engagement in or view of the organization to decline?
- If you were in my position, what is the first thing you would change?
- Are you willing to hang in for x amount of time to give me a chance to turn this around?

Listen intently to their answers and take notes. Once you have spoken to each person or department, compile the information, create a plan, and hold a full-staff video conference to roll out your morale development strategy. This might feel a little like political campaigning, but rather than looking at this as a race you really want to win, change your perception to look at it as a journey you want to take *with* your team. Your goal is to be the best you all can be—collectively and individually.

> The remote model at Lockwood allowed us to scale very quickly to meet our clients' objectives and hire the best talent. All of Lockwood's SOPs are based on a remote workforce and making sure our culture embraces this fact. We have embraced technology, which has clearly helped scale the organization. However, we also realize that live engagement is important, which is why we try to get teams live as much as possible.
>
> Some think that having remote teams is less expensive than having everyone come to an office. I would argue that it is a push at best, and most likely more expensive. Yes, you save money on real estate but if done correctly you spend at least as much on engaging the company with live events and so forth. In the end, I would not want to have it any other way.
>
> —Matthew Schecter,
> President and CEO, Lockwood

A Few More Thoughts

✓ **Be observant.** It is not often that a staff member will come to you and say, "Hey boss, morale is in the gutter." If you have a super open relationship and they feel comfortable doing that, then great! But more likely than not, this won't happen. So, it is up to you to observe the regular behaviors of your staff and notice when things are starting to shift in a downward direction. In a virtual setting, this might mean asking yourself some hard questions. Is there a staff member that typically chats you at least once a day, but has suddenly gone for days without a chat? Is there someone who is usually the first to speak up in a meeting but now there's nothing but radio silence? These are good indicators that something is amiss. Investigate.

✓ **Don't take it personally.** Shifts in morale are normal. If you're going through a lower season, remember that these things are part and parcel to every work environment. You're not the first to experience it. The key is to be proactive—figure it out and turn it around.

✓ **Remain open.** If you, as a manager, are closed off, you will never hear the valuable feedback that can help you refine your management skills. So, keep an open mind and invite your team to give constructive feedback. Empower them to be change agents in returning to a state of wonderful team morale.

✓ **Evaluate.** Once you get the morale turned around, it's important to evaluate all the information you gathered to figure out why morale fell in the first place. Was it a leadership issue? Is it something you need to look at within yourself? If you remain humble and can see within yourself the areas that need improvement—and then improve them—it will make maintaining good morale all that much easier.

Signing Off

Many of the things we've written about weave together and relate to other things in any form of workplace. Morale is no different. It is just that in the virtual workplace you need to respond more powerfully on the front and back ends, because the stuff in the middle is likely to get lost in a less stationary environment. More than ever you need to get comfortable on the phone and camera and work with your team to do the same.

If you take our advice on other areas contained within this book you will be well on your way to building or maintaining amazing morale within your organization. Ultimately, your staff wants to feel valued and respected. They want your investment in them to be at the same level as their investment in the organization. They want to be partners in the organization's success and recognized for their achievements. Seem like a tall order? If you work these things into your daily virtual managerial life, you'll find that it's simply your norm.

20.

Involving Outsiders: Special Guests, Speakers, and Third-Party Training

Making a guest feel welcome isn't hard, but it's extremely easy to unintentionally make them feel unwelcome. Especially in the workplace. And even more so in the virtual workplace.

When welcoming "outsiders" into your space, you can't stop at bringing the right level of enthusiasm or making sure you're on time; that's always really important. It's truly more about planning thoughtfully and thinking purposefully about who you are, who they are, and how the time they're going to spend with you and your team will be best experienced. When you've invited a special guest speaker or third-party trainer, you want to ensure the event goes off without a hitch.

Let's Level Set, Shall We?

When you invite someone into your home, you often provide a certain level of housekeeping for your guest: telling them your preference of shoes on or off in the house, showing them where the bathrooms are, and telling them in advance if you've got a dog or a cat or a whole menagerie.

You do this not only because it's polite, but because it's effective. You don't want dirty shoes on your carpet and you do want to know if your guests are allergic to cats or terrified of large snakes. You want them to feel comfortable and knowledgeable and at home in your home. And while this process isn't always followed in stationary workplaces—trust us, we've learned this firsthand—it's not only polite for the virtual workplace, it's downright essential for a variety of reasons.

You need to provide a certain level of introduction and housekeeping to your virtual guest speakers, trainers, and third parties because virtual office technology isn't learned in a day, let alone on the fly. So we'd like to introduce a few guidelines to make your next virtual guest—no matter what role they're playing—feel a warm welcome aimed for comfort and success. And look, we can't guarantee they'll be good at their jobs. But if you follow these tips, we can guarantee that you'll be known as a rock star to your staff and guest because at least you did your job well.

Create an Introductory Dossier

One of the best things you can create for any guest or speaker is a cheat sheet with some details and facts about your virtual workplace and team. It doesn't have to be some CIA-type overview, but just a quick reference to help guests learn a little about key features of their upcoming experience. It might include some of the following information:

- What technologies are you using? Do they need to register or are you offering any form of practice?

- How large is your team or guest list? Will participants be on mute the whole time? How will they be able to interact with your guest?

- Do you want to share any cultural norms or notes of distinction about your virtual workplace or employees? Perhaps you have a very lax culture, so people might be chatty. Or is there a possibility that people won't turn on their cameras, even though they know this is a video event? Should you warn them that because it's casual Friday everyone on camera could be wearing bunny pajamas? No matter what they might be, sharing these quirks is always a smart idea.

- Did you include a quick review of the day's agenda, their role, and the event's purpose? This is important because it allows your guests to track their plans against your needs.

Begin Introductions Much Earlier

You know how really sharp offices have that one person at the front desk that welcomes guests, offers them a drink, takes their coat, and makes them comfortable before their meeting, interview, or visit? That same concept can be easily replicated virtually. We recommend inviting your guest to join the session at least 15 minutes ahead of the planned event, no matter if it's on camera or conference line, so you can go over a variety of pre-event notes.

Make sure you:

- **Welcome them warmly.** Go over the event's agenda and any changes. Confirm their name and the correct pronunciation, and make sure they have your name and your organization's correct too.

- **Ask whether the introductory dossier you sent them helped.** Answer any questions they might still have.
- **Test the equipment.** Does their line sound clear? Do they know how to mute and unmute their line? Are you turning any controls over to them? If so, practice that and test the pass-off. Do they look good, clear, and well-lit on camera? If not, suggest a few tips and tweaks to make sure they look their best on camera.
- **Go over the initial agenda.** Explain that you'll be addressing some housekeeping issues (which we'll cover next) before you introduce them to begin the session.
- **Make them feel welcome.** Thank them again and invite them to take a moment to grab a glass of water before the event starts so they have it if they need it while speaking. Wait for them to return before opening the line or cameras to everyone else for the event.

Housekeeping Is Key

Once the line is open, the cameras are on, and you're about to get started, don't just launch into introductions. Take two minutes to go over a few housekeeping notes:

- Invite people to go on mute if necessary.
- Let people know if the session is being recorded, and where will it be it stored for later access.
- Remind folks how to best use the technology. Even if your team uses it every day, it's smart to go over those details because it also gives your guest a chance to hear them again.

- Address any planned interactions. Will there be any open lines or opportunities for questions, quizzes, or other engagement efforts?
- Mention if you have a backup plan. For example, what happens if there is lag or if the lines go down? Describe what to do next if any of these things happen—because they will. The best managers have a plan, express the plan, and then fulfill the plan.

Never Forget to Follow Up

How did it go? Was there too much housekeeping? Not enough? Did your guest have enough information to feel prepared and effectively plugged in? Did your team think the guest was prepared and fulfilled their role? Everyone deserves to share their side of the experience, so consider building a quick survey that your guests and your team can use to provide feedback. This also creates a nice way to thank everyone for their time.

A Few More Thoughts

✓ **Time is money.** Yes, we're asking you to consider building new tools, revisiting agendas, and carving out extra time ahead of the planned event; but in this case, the time you're pre-investing is time worth spending and will make everyone involved feel like a million bucks.

✓ **A manager's role is truly about multitasking to make things great.** Sure, you might want to exclusively focus on your guest's message, but even if you have an admin running the tech (moderating questions, keeping tabs on chatter, and so on) you need to focus on the overall experience. Pay attention to the details as the event progresses. Was the camera framed properly, and was the guest well-lit? If not, now you know to do it next time. Did the audio keep going out? Did people leave the call or video more often than you'd like? Was everyone silent? Refer back to your notes after the event to help determine how best to invest your efforts next time.

✓ **Thank your speaker.** Just as you took the time to tell them everything they needed to know on the front end, be sure to take the time to acknowledge their efforts and thank them on the back end. It's good practice to thank the speaker both publicly on camera at the end of the session, as well as more formally afterward. Perhaps send a thank you card or a carefully crafted email to thank them again for their time. Or cookies. Cookies always work.

Signing Off

Everyone wants to feel like their time was well spent. But that takes a certain level of housekeeping and event planning. In the virtual workplace there are too many variables to leave them all up to chance—the power might go out or someone's microphone might malfunction. You can't anticipate everything so make sure the stuff you can control—agendas, technology, housekeeping, warm welcomes, and thoughtful feedback efforts—is planned for and executed masterfully. Then use what you've built as a template for your future efforts (making any necessary tweaks along the way). These are the kinds of efforts that take a virtual manager from standard variety to exceptionally valued overnight.

21.

Birthdays, Happy Hours, and Holiday Parties

If you've worked in a stationary workplace you've probably found yourself in one of these situations: Packed into a break or conference room with all your co-workers, attempting idle chit-chat before singing happy birthday and eating cake; opening presents may or may not be involved. Or maybe it's the office party—often dreaded or highly anticipated, depending on who you are or whom you're celebrating. Or the (mandatory) office happy hour, which always seems to happen on your busiest day, but you can't skip because it'll look bad to your co-workers.

More times than you might think, we've been told by virtual workfolk that these experiences are either one of the things they miss the most or are the most thankful they don't have to experience any longer. Those who miss it, miss it because it's a form of workplace community and collegial engagement that's hard to replicate at Starbucks or with your household cats. *Trust us, Ben has tried and failed and has the scars and scratches to prove it.* They enjoy shaking things up by sharing a little casual conversation and a slice of cake with people they see every day but don't always get to interact with. On the other hand, some people are thankful they don't have to leave their desk or laptop for 20, 30, or 60 minutes to drink terrible punch, eat subpar sheet cake, and make idle chat-chat with co-workers they see every day, but don't actually *want* to interact with.

Let's Level Set, Shall We?

Essentially, some people see the glass half full, others half empty—with the glass in this analogy being a birthday, baby shower, work party, or happy hour, of course. Then there are others who don't see a glass at all, because if they've exclusively worked in the virtual world, they may never have gotten the chance. In this chapter, we offer a few thoughts on how to effectively adapt these moments of celebration in the virtual workplace, once and for all.

Birthdays and Baby Showers

Buying a cake for a stationary work event is easy. Someone does a headcount, calls a local bakery or grocery store, orders enough cake to feed said headcount, picks the cake up or has it delivered, cuts the cake, and serves the cake. All in all it's a four- to five-step process that just about anyone with access to the expense account, petty cash, or reimbursement form can handle. It may be a bit more complicated in a virtual work setting, but an absolutely doable process.

A budget for cake is a budget for cake, but that doesn't mean you can only order one cake that you literally have to cut up and serve to people in the breakroom. There are dozens of ways to bring "cake" or something festive to the doorstep of your virtual co-workers:

- **Allocate funding for cake.** Or not cake. It could be pie, soda, a cookie, pizza, vegan mac and cheese—whatever your preference. Set a small budget every month for your employees to buy their own celebratory edible to bring to the virtual party. Then you can indulge together while you sing happy birthday over a conference call or on camera. In lieu of setting a budget, you could send a virtual gift card or coupon.

- **Make it a free-for-all.** Invite everyone to bring their favorite cookie or snack to the event—a virtual potluck, if you will. Don't worry about providing funding or a budget, just make the experience relatable and fun by creating a theme everyone can support. Even better, let the individual having the birthday or baby shower choose the theme to personalize it for the occasion.

The virtual world has made it easier than ever to allow everyone to put in a few dollars collectively for a gift or gift card, which can then be sent virtually to the expectant parent or birthday boy or girl. Even the stationary worker has experienced this new convenience, so it's not a difficult one to organize in a virtual workplace.

The point is, the loss of a physical breakroom is no reason to stop celebrating people's life events. Get everyone on a conference call or video chat and spend 10, 20, or 30 minutes playing a game—like saying something nice about the birthday person or tossing out your favorite baby names—and sharing what you brought to the party (cake, cookies, hummus). There are endless ways to keep these parties cheap and simple, but also personal and fun.

Happy Hours

Of course, part of the fun of a happy hour is getting out of the office, running to the nearest bar, and blowing off some steam before heading home to keep talking about your co-workers with your family, spouse, or roommates. But happy hour is not a stationary-exclusive event. Here's how to plan a virtual one:

- **Set a time, date, and theme.** Are you all just trying to get to know one another? Looking to celebrate a recent win or soothe a recent struggle? Pick your theme, time, and date and treat this just like any other happy hour. Invite everyone to turn on their cameras and make it an after-work event so everyone can attend. Is your team a global one? If so, you might need host your happy hour later or earlier than usual (be sure to check out chapter 1 for more on navigating time zones). But that's OK because it's always five o'clock somewhere, right?

- **Make some mocktail and cocktail suggestions.** Once you've chosen your happy hour theme, come up with some drink suggestions that everyone can make, buy, or discuss. You can even share recipes. However, don't make them alcohol dependent, since some people might not drink or they just want another cup of coffee or glass of chilled water.

- **Plan how you'll meet.** Will you use your work phone or work video service? That's a possibility. But consider using a non-work-related service or provider instead. For one, it will not only feel more authentic to a happy hour experience—enjoying the company of co-workers away from work and work things—but it will also be a little more exciting to truly get away from work tools and tech.

- **Keep it short.** People naturally break off into groups during happy hours, coming and going as they please. A virtual happy hour deserves a different approach. Keep it to about 20 to 40 minutes. Any longer and it will begin to feel awkward and unnecessary. Invite everyone to be there at the start but let them know that they can leave whenever they'd like. Giving people the ability to just pop in, say hello, drink a drink, and then go about their evening is a wonderful way to virtually recreate a true happy hour experience.

- **Give it some structure.** Consider having someone "host" the happy hour. The host can be in charge of setting up some drinking games. Never Have I Ever is a classic— where folks say one thing they've never done, and then those who have done it take a sip of their drink. Another good game is Straight Face, where folks say something crazy, funny, or in a weird voice and anyone who laughs or smiles has to take a sip of their drink. The host can also end the evening by giving a brief toast to everyone having fun, getting to know one another, or the health and wealth of your organization.

Group Lunches, Ice Cream Socials, Secret Santa, and White Elephants

Finally, there are the smattering of work and holiday parties, which people inevitably either crave or truly can't stand. You know, the group lunches, themed parties, staff celebrations, and gift exchanges? Is there room for these in the virtual world? Of course. You just need to consider the same virtual vehicles and structure as any other virtual event—make it accessible to everyone involved, keep it simple and organized, and focus more on the culture or intent as the key feature.

If you want to host an ice cream social or group lunch event to celebrate the kickoff of summer or a new team milestone, just invite everyone to bring their favorite sandwich or pint of ice cream to your virtual meeting. Go around the room asking everyone what they're eating and what their favorite childhood version was growing up. Then, end with a toast to the celebration. Keep it quick (15 minutes should be plenty) so everyone can get back to their jobs.

If you're hosting a secret Santa, white elephant, or gift exchange, ask everyone to bring a gift that can be exchanged virtually, such as a gift card or online purchase. Again, keep it simple and short—schedule just enough time for everyone to share what they got and how they'll use it. And then get back to the grind. If you want to make things more exciting, you could add the gift exchange on to happy hour, but it's not necessary. Even just taking a 15-minute break to celebrate the gift of a co-worker's generosity can really brighten a day or make the week feel more festive.

A Few More Thoughts

✓ **Create a virtual party team.** The power of a party planning committee isn't just for stationary workplaces. Create a virtual one with people who love running smart, simple online events monthly or for special occasions. This is a great management tool, but an even better place for delegation.

✓ **Budget for morale.** Stationary or virtual, organizations with high employee engagement outperform those with low employee engagement by 202 percent (Katz 2017). So making room in your budget for employees to get coffee, cookies, or their own slice of cake can go a long way when it's connected to the opportunity to get on the phone or on camera for a small party or celebration.

✓ **Make it democratic.** Ask your employees if they want virtual opportunities for parties. Or host one or two virtual events and then take a poll on if they think they're worth their time. Don't just host these events because you can, do it because people appreciate them.

Signing Off

Make it fun, make it personal, make it virtually accessible. It's easy to just skip over conventionally stationary experiences like parties and celebrations, but why? Not only can they be just as fun—or more fun—virtually, they can be easier and far more painless. And as a manager of people, this is a perfect way to encourage team building that's easy to organize and simple to experience. The virtual workplace doesn't have to be cold or distant; warm things up with traditional gatherings, set to the tune of a virtual landscape.

22.

Cliques

Think back to your time in junior high or high school, or check out the movie *Mean Girls*. You probably still remember what cliques your school had and who were in them. Even as adults, we still experience cliques every day, whether we're part of one or are on the outside longing to get in.

In a stationary workplace, you can imagine what this looks like. The word "clique" alone evokes images of four office friends enjoying their private Wine Club Wednesdays (wine and cheese for lunch), whispering among themselves, laughing at inside jokes, and being weird and awkward around other co-workers. Are they just having a good time? Are they talking about everyone else? Why are none of us invited anyway? No matter the situation, it's gross and juvenile.

This is one of those things that could be more difficult to detect in the virtual workplace, but it's just as dangerous. Virtual cliques can quickly become cancerous, so you need to learn to keep an eye out for them. There is pretty much nothing you can do about people becoming close and forming relationships with one another. In fact, you want that to happen on your virtual team. But when it starts to become an exclusive club or "*Mean Girl*-ish," that's when it becomes risky business.

Let's Level Set, Shall We?

How about we get one thing out of the way: Not all cliques are bad. In fact, the part about a small group of people who want to spend time together is usually a good thing. People do that every day. It's healthy, and it's normal. Until it's not. Because, you see, cliques also have a tendency to identify people they do not want in their group—the "us four and no more" mentality. And this is precisely why the word "clique" is rarely used with a positive connotation.

Virtual Cliquery

What do cliques look like in a virtual world? And how do you address the problem when they form? We have a few thoughts on the subject for virtual managers.

Banding Together in Meetings

If you start to notice that certain people are banding together in your meetings—speaking for each other or trying to help explain each other's points, especially if discussion gets heated—it's a good indication that a clique has formed.

Offline Agreements

When someone is always offering advice such as, "I discussed this with so-and-so and we agree that…" it's a fantastic indication that a clique has formed. When people are discussing things with their peers before they discuss them with you, they've likely formed a relationship that could turn into a clique if it hasn't already.

Giggles Without Jokes

If you are having a virtual meeting and one or more of your staff start to engage in telling jokes or stories that only a couple others know about or can relate to, this is another indicator of potential cliquism. Keep an eye out for people making inside jokes or telling inside stories while in meetings or laughing at things that seem to have no natural root in the conversation.

Addressing Cliques Indirectly

Addressing something as subtle as cliques in a workplace—and a virtual workplace at that—is an interesting endeavor indeed. It's not like you can just forcefully point a finger at someone and yell *"Clique!!! Burn them!"* because that's crazy and also inappropriate. But there are some things you can preemptively do before it becomes a real issue.

Emphasize the Importance of Teamwork

You will find more suggestions in the chapter on team building, but take the opportunity in meetings to reiterate the importance of working as a team to get the job done. Or schedule some sort of team building session to really drive the point home.

Review Policies

From time to time it's not a bad idea (even aside from the clique issue) to review policies with your staff. Remind them that work equipment is to be used for work only. Hopefully they will start to understand that their clique business doesn't belong and shouldn't continue.

Spend Time With Suspected Clique Members

No, don't "join" the group. Simply spending a little extra time with those you suspect are part of the clique could go a long way toward dissolving it. Chat or call them individually and ask them how things are going. Let them talk, and listen well. It might be that they are simply frustrated with some aspect of the job and are looking for others to accept and commiserate with them.

A Few More Thoughts

✓ **Look deeper.** A clique is made up of two parts: people spending time together and people who don't want anyone else in the group. Naturally, people want to spend time together because they hold common views about a particular person or thing. In this space, it's likely a particular view on the workplace. Dig into that a little bit. Look beneath the surface, understanding that in this environment, it likely started because someone was unhappy. Refer to the chapter on morale for ways to address the happiness issue.

✓ **If all else fails, address it directly.** If someone in your organization is becoming problematic because they are involved in a clique or are its leader, you will need to address that. If you tried to indirectly deal with it before it became a real problem, and the problem just got worse, you have to address it head on. The last thing you want or need is for a clique to grow in magnitude and unhappiness toward another person, because it has the potential to turn into harassment or bullying.

Signing Off

You might not be able to come right out and say "you guys are in a clique and it needs to stop now," but with your virtual manager superpowers you will be able to spot a clique from a mile away (or from around the globe) and leap to your team's rescue with a single bound. Understand that cliques can start out innocently enough, but could easily turn into something much uglier, such as harassment or bullying (see our chapter on this), if not addressed. Remember—you are responsible for your entire team. So do what you know is best for the group as a whole and take the steps you need to stop the progression of ugly clique behavior.

23.

Gossip, News, and Lies

No matter what you've heard—or who you heard it from—the digital watercooler is just as refreshing as the stationary water-cooler when it comes to issues such as sharing office gossip, news, and misunderstandings or lies among employees. Much of the communications that take place in the virtual workplace are over mediums like email and IM. So people are no longer just discussing gossip, news, and lies in hushed tones at the water cooler—now what they're saying can be seen and heard, and it's even harder to keep it a secret.

Let's Level Set, Shall We?

As a manager, how you tackle issues such as spreading work-place gossip, news, and misunderstandings is one of those less-talked-about skills that can make or break your success.

About a year into my first nonprofit job, my department was moved under an entirely new, larger department. It was a rocky fit. And at the time, I was an out gay man with friends and family, but I wasn't yet out at work. The new department head asked her admin to send an email asking a whole host of questions so she could "get to know us better," but the questions were weird—asking if we were married or had kids, where we lived in the city, and so on.

I responded via email and politely declined to answer any of it, explaining that I didn't think it was necessary to get to know me. Within seconds the admin was in my doorway looking red and anxious, apologizing profusely. Slightly confused, I looked down at my inbox and saw that she had sent me a snarky message stating "What a jerk. He just doesn't want people to know he's totally gay." It was clearly intended for some co-worker friend of hers. And while I don't know where that young lady is today, she didn't last much longer at that company. Gossip like this, spread via email, can permeate stationary and virtual workplaces alike.

—Ben

Gossip

As famous American journalist, gossip columnist, and author Earl Wilson once said, "Gossip is when you hear something you like about someone you don't." And it's often considered a workplace staple. But it doesn't have to be.

As a virtual manager the tact, transparency, and culture you create for your team is often just as important as—if not more important than—how you're expected to deal with gossip. The following are a few things you can think about.

Create a Culture of Transparency

While it can take any form, office gossip is often based on poor organizational or managerial decision making and communications. One of the best things you can do is provide a place where people can trust you, trust your management, and trust the culture you've created for your employees, team, and department. This means working hard to be clear, concise, and focused in your approach. Aim to have transparency and accountability in your work and create safe, trusting spaces for people to express themselves, their concerns, and their general grievances.

Create a Culture of Deflation

Gossip will happen, so don't avoid the topic or turn a blind eye or ear when it happens. Whenever you see it, hear it, or hear of it, go straight to the source via phone or video to diffuse it and deflate the rumor. We've said it before and we'll say it again, video is the best option for this conversation. Yes, it'll be awkward and it's not fun, and it might make you look like a wet blanket to certain employees, but those are the kinds of employees you probably need to keep an extra eye on anyway. You shouldn't care what they think.

When gossip is spread, and you've already fostered a culture of transparency, you need to reinforce the nature and purpose of that culture to everyone involved by talking to them on the phone or video. If you haven't fostered that culture yet, now is as good a time as any to build that plan and create the transparency necessary to avoid these problems in the future.

News and Misunderstandings

Every organization has news or announcements. And the ways in which they choose to share that news with individual employees or organizationally will change, depending on what's being done and who is affected. Sometimes, something that's earmarked as "gossip" but is in fact true—like information about like organizational job cuts, bonuses, or unapproved budgets—will slip out in advance even if it's not meant to be shared with another team or department. Keep the following tips in mind when sharing news.

The Medium Matters

As a manager, remind your employees how news is shared in your virtual workplace. Will it be an interoffice memo? An all-company email? A virtual town hall? No matter the method, you need to remind them that if they hear something that is not coming from one or more of the acceptable methods of disbursement, they need to come to you for clarity or assurance.

Don't Let It Run Free

This is no different from the issue of dealing with outlying gossip. Don't avoid the topic and don't turn a blind eye or ear when it happens. When you see it, hear it, or hear of it, go straight to the source via phone or video. It's your job as a manager to actually manage the situations at hand. Again, it's not fun, it can be awkward, but no one said management was a cake walk.

A Few More Thoughts

✓ Don't get caught with your hand in the cookie jar.
   When you're in an organizational leadership role, like management, you will be placed in a variety of situations to learn information early. Most of it will be news. Some could be lies. And even some might be gossip-worthy. But don't abuse your role by gossiping or sharing news too

early. You don't want to be the one having a phone or video meeting about questions concerning your behavior. You think the reverse is awkward? Try being on the receiving end.

✓ **Don't dole out repercussions unless there is disregard.** There is a massive line between someone telling you someone else is sharing gossip and the person sharing the gossip. Don't get them confused. You want to create a culture of trust and open communications. That starts with ensuring no repercussions when an employee trusts you enough to take you at your word to talk with you when someone is spreading gossip, news, or lies.

✓ **Take corrective action when necessary.** Spreading gossip, news, or lies isn't just an insular problem, it can also hit at a larger toxic-culture problem. It's your job to get to the bottom of the situation. Don't take these issues so lightly you're just brushing them off—simply talking about it with the perpetrator is not enough. You need to correct the action because the problem is an indicator of larger behaviors that could tear any workplace down, and really get into the nooks and crannies of a virtual workplace.

Signing Off

Management isn't always caviar dreams and screaming "I'm on a boat" while sipping champagne. Nope, sometimes it's catching an email where someone is talking inappropriately about another employee or the organization. Or it's having someone send you a link to a video call where someone is prematurely sharing organizational news or spreading lies about leadership. In these moments you need to disembark from the yacht and schedule a phone call or video chat with the employees in question to get to the bottom of the issue, make sure it doesn't happen again, and potentially write up anyone deserving. (See the chapter on disciplinary meetings.) It's not fun or glamorous, but it is an important part of being a good manager who works hard to create cultures of transparency and accountability.

24.

Best Benefits: Soda, Coffee, Field Trips, and Volunteerism

When people hear we've worked in both stationary and virtual workplaces, they always ask us which is better. And we always say it depends on the employee, the organization, and the topic at hand. And even then, it's usually still split down the middle. As you've seen, it's rarely about which is "better" and more about how things are tackled.

If you catch us on the right day, we'll quietly admit that one wins over the other on certain topics. This chapter represents one. Like it or not, when it comes to things organizations offer—like free snacks and drinks; various working, napping, or gaming setups; or even field trips and group volunteer events—stationary has it on lock. But that's changing.

Let's Level Set, Shall We?

One of the exciting things about a writing a book like this is that we get to take every topic you can think of and apply it to the virtual world. Some topics were boring, like chapter 11's "How do you best handle virtual performance reviews?" and others were juicier, like chapter 28's "How do you deal with interoffice virtual romance?" But this also gave us license to consider bigger-picture topics that, at first glance, seem completely unrealistic in the virtual setting. Can you virtually replicate free snacks and drinks? Is there such a thing as offering video games, ball pits, and napping pods in a virtual workplace? How do you create employee engagement efforts like group volunteerism or field trips?

Well, we love a challenge, so we're devoting this chapter to those of you who think bigger, act bolder, and know that with the right budget and a little creativity, nothing is impossible.

Fair warning: Some of these you could advocate for or tackle as a manager, while others will require a higher power. But we thought we'd start somewhere!

Free Snacks and Drinks

We admit that stocking one or more virtual employees with free water, coffee, tea, soda, or beer and snacks is extraordinarily difficult, if not impossible. One or more stationary workplaces, sure, but individual people? No chance. But we'd also argue that you're thinking far too literally. Here are some solutions:

- **Create a drink and snack stipend.** You don't have to worry about what everyone, anyone might want to eat or drink if you aren't responsible for the details. Offer all employees a set amount of money per paycheck or a reimbursable option for snacks. Or maybe you've got a company portal they can use to buy snacks and drinks online while they're working at their own home or from a virtual office. Let them decide if they want fancy bottled water or locally produced sour apple kombucha. Just make it available for them to make their own choices.

- **Send digital coupons or gift cards.** Once a month or during the holidays, send your virtual employees a gift card they can use to buy drinks and snacks.
- **Literally send them snacks and drinks.** Send a small supply of snacks and drinks to their doorstep every week or month. It's not as flexible as the first option, but just about everyone would benefit from the gift. It's like the ultimate subscription box!

Video Games, Creative Workstations, and Napping Pods

All the fancy start-ups offer them—fun rooms filled with toys and nostalgia, places to nap, and standing or treadmill desks in forest-like, Astroturf-laden or hyper-modern, rock concert atmospheres. How on earth can your virtual office compete with that? Here's how:

- **Offer personal budgets for office and atmospheric enhancements.** Does your employee want a ball chair? Hoping for a standing desk? Give everyone an office enhancement budget with pre-identified or approved lists of items they can order.
- **Video games live online too, you know.** You don't need to send each employee a woodgrain 1982 Ms. PacMan game console. Instead host online games! There are endless solo and group games online

you could offer through a portal on your company intranet. That way folks can game at their leisure without worrying how they're going to fit an air hockey table in their dining room.

- **Who needs a pod?** They have beds in their homes. If you were going to offer napping pods or free chair massages in a stationary office, you can easily allow employees to schedule 30 minutes a week for a nap or massage. And bonus, you don't even need to offer payment for these things, just allow the time to enjoy the treatment or, better yet, sleepment (we had to).

Group Volunteerism

Giving people PTO for volunteerism is quickly becoming a new norm in any work setting. Virtual is no different. But if you're trying to recreate some form of group experience, that can be trickier.

Fortunately, volunteering is becoming increasingly virtual. Many national and global organizations offer individual and group online volunteer opportunities. Here are just a few to consider looking into:

- **Missing Maps Project.** Virtual groups help provide land-mapping tools, where volunteers work in teams to review satellite topographical maps and create open street maps for vulnerable communities.
- **Thank you banks.** Virtual groups help nonprofits thank donors and other volunteers through phone and email banks.
- **Mass research and admin projects.** Virtual groups help nonprofits and charities with large-scale research, analysis, data, and database projects and maintenance.

Field Trips

In many ways the virtual world has helped shrink what was once a very large physical world. Popular games like Pokémon Go, for example, can be played outdoors in groups. Here are some other ideas to consider:

- **Discover Discovery.** Discovery Education is a great online resource that allows "students" to go beyond the classroom into virtual groups to explore uncharted and well-known areas of the planet without leaving their desktop.

- **Visit your art or area museum, together.** Have your employees head to their favorite local museum (or park or wetland or mall) and lead 10-minute tours on camera of their favorite parts of the place.

I was planning a meeting one year that would take place in Dublin, Ireland. I had completed my site visits and chosen the venue, and everything was pretty well set. Just days before I left for the meeting, the venue event manager emailed me that she wanted to show me another idea about how to set up our main meeting space. We decided the easiest thing to do was jump on a video call. Once connected, she walked me through the venue showing a couple ways she had set up other spaces. Then she took me into the main room, where the event staff had set up half the room in one style and the other half in the other style, so I could get a good visual and make a final decision. This was such a clever way to quickly understand what she was talking about and come to a speedy decision. It was also so nice to be able to take a little field trip to Ireland in the middle of my day.

—Kathy

A Few More Thoughts

✓ **Think outside the box.** Here are a couple more ideas from well-known companies that you can ponder for your team:

- Shut down the company (with pay) for the week between Christmas and New Year.
- Offer employees a fixed amount of money each year to donate to the charity of their choice.
- Provide subscriptions to audiobook services or electronic readers as well as a book a month so your staff can continue learning and growing.
- Offer unpaid monthlong sabbaticals employees can use for any reason.
- Offer three- to six-month sabbaticals paid out at 40 percent of the employee's salary, which they can use to pursue personal or professional growth opportunities.
- Provide the option for pet health insurance—we all want our furry friends, who we're with almost all the time when we're working from home, to be in top-notch health.

✓ **Offer wellness stipends, gym memberships, or fitness trackers to your staff**—then hold internal competitions to build health and rapport!

Signing Off

There is a method of critical thinking called the HMW Question Method that we love. HMW stands for "How might we . . ." thoughtfully unravel problems or given situations. As a manager or leader of your organization, use this method every time you see a stationary workplace perk or benefit that you think is cool, but seems impossible to replicate in the virtual world. In some cases, it might be. Like an office ball pit. Although even if it's possible, it may not be worth attempting—like an office ball pit.

And remember, lot of these perks are really gravy on the virtual workplace heap of mashed potatoes. What beats being able to wear pajamas in your home office with your own pets just steps away from your own bed? Not much. So the virtual workplace has some pretty darn good perks that are hard to replicate in the stationary world.

When you do see a perk that's worth converting for the digital world, try it out. And then let us know how it went. We'd love to feature yours in a future edition of the book or online!

HOME VS. OFFICE

Addressing
Procedure With
(or Without)
a Policy

25.
Laundry, Cooking, and Running Errands

There are two things you can be guaranteed to hear when someone learns you work from home: First they'll say something like, "It must be so nice to not have to worry about showering or having to dress normal," which is always odd to hear. Sure, you might wear pajama bottoms more often than not, but it's not like you avoid the shower for days on end, relishing in not having to stay clean.

The second thing you'll hear usually sounds something like, "Oh, how great is it to do a load of laundry while taking a meeting, or being able to just run out to pick up a prescription and no one's the wiser?" It's always asked like a question, but it's meant as a statement. And as such, you'll usually respond with a light laugh and say something like "Oh, totally." Because that's often not true at all. Or maybe it *is* totally true, but it's also none of their daily-showered-dress-clothes-cubicle-dwelling business.

So what's the point of a chapter devoted to laundry, cooking, and running errands? Guidance! When it comes to their own interests and the interests of their employees, it's time for virtual managers to stop pretending it's some weird, unspoken secret.

> *I think the phrase "working from home" creates the sense that people aren't actually working as hard as they could be or perhaps not even working at all. Part of this theory might stem from the fact that most people who work from home do so in yoga pants or pajamas. Does it really matter? Because the dress code at home is casual, does that mean the level of work output is also casual, or can you put your best foot forward in a robe and slippers? Have you ever seen a head shot of a Fortune 500 CEO in anything less than a suit and tie? Is there a good reason for this? Should we expect that the term "dress for success" apply to all scenarios to dismantle the theory that a casual outfit leads to casual output? Does business attire ultimately impact how we operate? If not, why have suits or uniforms historically been such a large investment in the corporate world? Should office attire apply at your home office too?*
>
> —Michelle Polinko, Chief Development Officer, Northeast Ohio Region of the American Red Cross

Let's Level Set, Shall We?

Just because you're working from home, does that mean you should get the liberty to do a few loads of laundry or run the occasional quick errand to pick up some sugar or a prescription at your leisure? Yes. But also maybe, no. In brief, it's very much dependent on the circumstances of your office culture and organizational policies. There are so many ways that this topic is inadequately addressed or defined for virtual teams. It's a perfect microcosm for why we wrote this book.

You Can Have It All, and Smell Spring Fresh Too

Do a load of laundry. Throw it in before your first call of the day, take two minutes a few hours later to toss it in the dryer, and then fold it and put it all away during lunch. Why not? However, if you or your employees are alternating between answering emails and attending meetings while sorting, washing, drying, folding, and putting away *several* loads of laundry a day, we call foul. The time behind all of that would add up and it's encroaching on workplace neglect. Don't give us all a bad name! So, while you shouldn't open a laundromat in your house, doing one, maybe two, loads throughout the week? Sure.

If it's done smartly, doing something like a load of laundry shouldn't have any more impact on your virtual job than the random breaks folks take in a proximity workplace, like hanging in a co-worker's cubicle to catch up, taking trips to the watercooler, or maybe sneaking into the breakroom to check out the donut situation.

In fact, giving this advice to your employees is not only liberating but another way to express the benefits and realities of virtual employment. Why would we turn a blind eye? This could be a smart, fun anecdote to use during the orientation and onboarding process: "Oh, and yes, you can do a load of laundry in between day-to-day duties here at Company XYZ, just don't make it a daily habit or have it obstruct any part of your planned day, please."

You Can Cook Your Lunch, and Eat It Too

Working virtually opens up the opportunity to be home for your lunch hour—your *full* lunch hour—in a way that just isn't available when working in a traditional office. Depending on the type of person you are, you might find this more or less difficult than being in an office setting. When working from home, gone are the days of running out the door in a frenzy and forgetting your lunch, only to have to buy lunch later, spending way more than you should. Or perhaps you find eating lunch at home a bit like looking at the menu of a Jersey diner—everything you could possibly desire is there and it's impossible to choose because everything sounds good.

The best tip we can give you on this is to plan. Just as if you were going into an office, choose what you will have for lunch the night before and set it aside so it's easy to access when lunch time rolls around. We went back and forth about whether this chapter should be filled with tips on how to better plan for lunch, and we did come up with a few:

- Prep your lunch the night before.
- Buy easier meals to make in your microwave or straight out of the fridge.
- Don't forget that many restaurants deliver just about everywhere.
- Who needs lunch, anyway?

But then we realized that this book is built to answer questions about things you can't find on Google, and there are a million ways to search for fast tips for lunch at home or on the go. So we decided to take an entirely different approach: Don't overlook the importance of lunch in any workplace—virtual or stationary—and remind your employees the very same.

Taking an hour to step away from your desk is important. Especially in an environment where you might not leave your house for days at time if you didn't have a reason to leave. So, get up, get away from your desk, and make your lunch. Eat on your porch or balcony or at the park across the street. Or maybe go out to eat, but do it somewhere nearby so you don't go over your time.

Just like in the proximal workplace, you can also use your break to do other things, like take a brisk 20-minute walk or grab a first or second shower. Use the time to chat with friends or family or spend time with your pets or kids or tackle a few chores. Be in the moment and around others, away from work, and engaged in anything but work. Let your lunch hour be a little reminder in the middle of your workday that you're more than just a face in front of a set of monitors and keyboards.

> *Taking time away from your computer during your work day is such an important part of your own overall wellbeing. On a nice day, I sometimes go on a quick trail walk over my lunch break—15-minute drive, 30-minute walk, 15-minute drive back. It energizes me for the rest of the day and helps me get a little extra physical activity.*
>
> *Also, a few friends who also work virtually meet at my house a couple times a week and we work together. Sometimes we take our lunch break to chat and catch up with one another, or maybe I'll make lunch for all of us, or sometimes we go out to eat somewhere local. Whatever the lunch plan is for the day, I always make sure I take that crucial time to mentally break from my work and reset for the afternoon.*
>
> *—Kathy*

Out of Office, Out of Mind?

Errands. Whether you're going to the store for milk, the pharmacy for medicine, or the dry cleaners to get things pressed, errands are little micro trips that you take once or several times based on your needs. When done over your lunch break, who knows, who cares, and what does it matter? However, outside that timeframe, we think it's a different story. Unlike a load of laundry—which one might argue is a micro-errand within the home itself—running errands outside the home is a whole different issue. And yes, we realize that most of your work can probably be done from your smartphone, so you may think there's no harm in running an errand or two if you have time to spare and no one will notice. Well, from your own perspective, maybe not much. But when you consider this through the lens of being a manager, you might feel a little different.

Remember the chapter about flexible schedules, where we talked about how flexibility is not only beneficial but often essential? One way to think about errands is to focus on how or where they need to get done within the time and space of your day. Meaning that while some errands might be more important than others, broadly speaking, we don't think this is a perk or privilege you should exercise consistently without acknowledgment or permission from a boss or supervisor.

As always, our advice about policies and procedures is warranted here too, but this also becomes another topic about culture and disclosure. If you're fine with virtual employees running the occasional errand with permission— let that be known and clear. It's a wonderful stance to have, and it will be appreciated and welcomed. But if you're not, let that be known and clear too. It might not be as wonderful or welcome, but it will still be appreciated and respected.

Yep. I do chores at work—the kind of chores that don't require much focus, attention, or work, but might take some time. I put laundry in the washer before I start the day, I move it to the dryer mid-morning, and I sometimes fold it during lunch. More often than not, there's a gigantic pile of clean laundry in our living room for my husband when he gets home from work. Somedays I chop up vegetables and toss them in the slow cooker in the morning. It takes about 10 minutes, and then when my day's over, I have dinner ready for my family. And other days, I use my lunch break (when I actually take it) to run to the grocery store, post office, or pharmacy. Being OK with this might be the biggest shift, from both my vantage point as an employee and supervisor. I liken it to the time spent chatting at another colleague's desk or running out for coffee during the workday.

—Rachael Orose, Vice President of a National Nonprofit

A Few More Thoughts

✓ **Keep an eye on the time.** Making your lunch (soup, a sandwich, or some pasta) is a far cry from baking a pie or preparing a roast and vegetables. While we'd never put an actual time clock on your prep, if you're taking longer to make something than you would spend at your table in a restaurant, it's likely bordering on an inappropriate use of time.

Signing Off

Are stationary employees truly under the thumb of their employer by design or default? Just because you can often "see" them, does that mean their culture is truly different? Maybe. Does being virtual, and thereby not often being "seen," allow you to be less under watch? Again, maybe. But does that mean the opportunities are truly ripe for employees to do what they please and go where they want, when they want, on company time and dime? No!

That being said, working from home does change the landscape of opportunity, need, and privilege. Therefore, topics like doing laundry, taking time to cook a meal, and running errands are worthy of real conversations about real conditions and expectations.

As a manager of virtual employees, the topics and experiences are different, and as such should be handled differently. The trick here, like every topic we cover, is to be real, honest, direct, and open. Because if you're not, it's really easy to not just lose focus of the realities of the virtual workplace, but also to lose track of your people.

26.

Taking Meetings
on the Toilet

We've all done it. And even if you've never done it *wink* I can promise you that just about anyone you've worked with virtually has taken a meeting on the toilet.

It might not have been the entire meeting—heaven forbid—but at least long enough to get that second job done. So what? Some people aren't even wearing pants while they work from home. Who cares if they're taking a meeting about one thing while doing number two?

Honestly, that depends on who you are. This chapter offers a little bit for everyone to make sure that if you do ever need to perform that duty, you're doing it right. We could just tell you "don't do it!" but we're nothing if not optimistic realists. This chapter is the least we can do.

Let's Level Set, Shall We?

When we say this chapter is for *everyone*—we do mean *everyone*. And no, not just because as you've undoubtedly heard, "everybody poops," but because we realize that sometimes there is a fine line between doing something truly wrong and doing something wrong truly effectively. Meaning, unless you have an explicit policy prohibiting the use of the bathroom while on a business or conference call—something we address and support later in this chapter for those who need that level of endorsement—then one of the best things we can do is express how to do something terrible well.

The Three Types of Work-From-Homers

When it comes to taking meetings or calls on the toilet, we've noticed people typically fall into one of three buckets:

- **The "I Would Never. I Will Never." crowd.** Our advice to this group boils down to *hello, welcome to your first day of virtual management.* Or maybe more accurately, *good for you, noble bladder-holder!* You are a true unicorn and we bow to you. Keep doing what you're not doing.

- **The "I Have and I Promise to Never Do It Again" group.** Look, we've all been there. In a standard conference room meeting, you'll see someone excuse themselves with no reason and return a few moments later with cleaner hands and no one bats an eyelash. But virtually, it can be a little more complicated. Can you discretely excuse yourself on a conference call? Not really. It's much more tempting to just sneakily press mute for 60-90 seconds and hope you're not called on to give a comment or feedback. Don't beat yourself up about it.

- The unabashed "I Do. I Have. And I Most Certainly Will Again" team. Of course you have. And of course you will. Thank you for being honest.

Steps to Do It Right

Assuming that you don't fall into the first group, or you do but you manage a team who identifies with the second or third group, what are you supposed to do? Let's really talk about how to do this right:

1. **Put. Your. Phone. On. Mute.** Don't cover the microphone. Don't walk away from the phone. Press mute, do your business, flush, wash your hands, and then unmute. Don't do that freshman move of unmuting before you wash your hands. No one is going to believe that you're just washing a quick dish or randomly just washing your hands? Once anyone hears the water flowing, they will know what you did.

2. **Try to avoid talking in your bathroom.** Have you ever listened to your voice in your bathroom compared with any other room in your house? Most bathrooms are small, painted in eggshell or a high-gloss paint, and filled with metal, porcelain, glass, tile, mirrors, and other vocally reflective materials. When you're in the bathroom, your voice will sound shiny and like you're talking in a tin echo chamber. It is extremely obvious that you're in a different room, and someone will wonder why. Don't make them wonder. Avoid the wondering.

3. **Don't attempt number 2 when you're number 1 on the call.** If you are an essential member of the conference call, don't get bold. Don't think that no one will notice

you've disappeared for several minutes or more. You may be able to bluff yourself out of this one, but only once, and it's more likely you'll get flustered, which will only add to the confusion and guilt. Trust us.

4. **Don't attempt this during one-on-one calls.** Maybe you've been using the bathroom on conference calls and webinars for years. You've built up not only skills, but confidence. Don't get cocky. These days it's really easy to tell if someone has been put on mute. And taking yourself off mute when the person you're meeting with says "Hello, Susan, are you there?" might reveal a little more than just your voice responding with "Yep, right here."

5. **Nature calls and I must answer.** As a last resort (or maybe a first resort?) just as people excuse themselves for a few moments in a physical meeting, that is always an option on a conference call too. Sometimes nature calls at inconvenient times, and there's nothing you can do about it. However, you always have the option to politely excuse yourself and then return to the conference when you're done. If it's a video conference, perhaps you create a policy to simply turn your camera off when you need to be excused, rather than interrupt the meeting with an announcement that you'll be right back.

What About Your Employees?

So what is the best defense against having your employees break this unstated rule of thumb? A policy and procedure approach, naturally. It's as simple as saying "Please don't use the bathroom while on a work call."

Discussing bathroom breaks at the workplace can be awkward and embarrassing. However, as OSHA points out, there are real laws governing bathroom breaks and it's often a necessary communication to have and outline between employers and employees. And it shouldn't be a free-for-all just because you're in a virtual environment.

So developing a policy that states that employees should respect the virtual experience and refrain from using the bathroom—even while using a mute feature or any of our awesome tips—while on calls is smart. This way, if someone is caught using the bathroom while on a call, you can address it as a true policy issue, not as a preference or cultural one. It's one thing to suggest business shouldn't be conducted from the toilet as policy, it's another to just be crappy about it because you think you heard a toilet flush.

A Few More Thoughts

✓ **Don't attempt to normalize this topic.** Even if everyone uses the advice we've given on the subject, that doesn't mean everyone is comfortable discussing it. Don't think that just because everyone does it, that means anyone wants to talk about it openly or otherwise.

✓ **Use discretion.** This topic, like any other potentially difficult or disciplinary topic, should not be discussed on a group call if delinquent action is suspected. Anything that should or could be discussed should be done so with discretion and tact.

Signing Off

You might be laughing right now, or perhaps you're crying. This chapter alone might have been the very reason you purchased this book! The reason this topic is so seemingly taboo and fascinating is because it's an extremely unique one within the world of the virtual workplace. Plus, it's not too foreign to understand—research has found that somewhere between 38 and 75 percent of people anonymously admit to the dirty little habit of using their phone or tablet on the toilet anyway (Rivers 2016). So even if you've never been there personally, you can understand the gravity of this modern utilization of mobile technology.

Like any difficult topic, it's one you can effectively ignore until you can't any longer. However, the knowing echo of a stall, the sound of flush, or the strange intermittent muting with no explanation can cause an assumption or realization that makes us all feel uncomfortable. What happens next is up to you. Do you have enough evidence to address the issue? Do you have a policy that prohibits the activity? If not, some things are better left unsaid and unexplored. We suggest you flush that topic away quietly, preferably while on mute.

27.

Puppies, Kitties, and Children

Do you remember the 2017 video of Dr. Robert Kelly, the British professor who, while being interviewed in his home office on South Korean politics for BBC World News, was interrupted on camera by his adorable two children and then his frantic wife who was trying to gather said children? It went viral, and everyone who was anyone saw it within a few weeks.

If you were someone who worked from home, it went a little more than viral, it went mildly cancerous. Friends, family, and co-workers alike sent dozens of links to the incident with remarks like, "OMG has this ever happened to you?" or "Something to think about!" We know this from experience, because we received a link to Dr. Kelly's video more than fifty times in just two days. Our personal favorite comment was, "You don't have any kids, but any one of your many cats could do this, so make sure to lock your door!"

Let's Level Set, Shall We?

The video brought to light an issue that often plagues the minds of remote workers: What happens if my husband or wife, children or pets, parents or roommates just casually walk into frame while I'm conducting a meeting? Just as you might worry about your phone going off in a crowded theater, the concerns surrounding how working from home plays out in any number of situations are real.

As addressed earlier in the chapter about privacy, working remotely requires an extra layer of discretion and planning. However, in this chapter, we want to cover a topic is that fairly unique to the modern remote worker and manager: letting people into your world, into your home, and into your home office, as a daily part of your employment. Whether they're heard over the phone or seen on video chat, parts of your private life are often on display, and that often includes anyone or anything that lives with you.

On one hand, you want to be mindful that a loved one, roommate, or pet could interrupt a meeting or call, but there is another side to the equation: When your co-workers *want* to see your new kitten or puppy. Or they want to say hello to your children who are home because of a holiday break or time-difference. Or they want to say a hello to your husband or wife because they are also at home.

What does one do? Build a set of policies related to the inclusion and exclusion of family members, pets, and interruptions.

Creating Policy From or For Potential Chaos

Life happens. No one knows this better than the aforementioned Dr. Kelly, who came to be known as "BBC Dad," but that doesn't mean you shouldn't anticipate life and try to prepare for it. In a modern, virtual word, we propose a few pointers, policies, and procedures related to the existence of what we like to call *Virtphy's Law*—a virtual riff on the term *Murphy's Law,* meaning anything that can go wrong in your virtual setting will go wrong.

Lock Your Doors

Lock your doors and remind those you manage to do the same. It's that simple. Suggest hanging a dry erase board or posting a note on the door so folks on the other side know why the door is shut and locked, and why they shouldn't knock, jiggle the handle, or yell through the door asking why it's locked in the first place:

> *"In a one-hour meeting."*
> *"On a client call."*
> *"Do not disturb."*
> *"Anyone who enters will be asked to dance on camera for my co-workers."*

Any of these messages should be enough to make adults and most kids stay quiet and respectful around your closed, locked door. It's also thoughtful and kind. If you're not always home alone when working, letting those who live with you have a small level of insight to your day or how they should or shouldn't conduct themselves while you're working is just showing respect in both directions.

Don't forget that a locked door is often truly just an invitation to knock. But a locked door with a smart note is golden.

Post a Calendar

While it's possible to get sucked into a meeting or call at any moment, it's safe to say that at least 50 percent of your day is probably pre-scheduled. And while your co-workers and direct reports often have access to your calendar—at least to see what's blocked off—it doesn't hurt to do the same for your household.

Creating a virtual shared calendar is easy, and modern technology allows you to merge your work calendar with another calendar that you can share anyone else. Or in a pinch, you could just post a handwritten or printed calendar on your door to share what your day looks like and when you need privacy. Just make sure to remind those you manage do not *directly* share their work calendar with a friend or loved one; most workplace email systems won't allow third-party emails to do so, but in case they do, have a policy in place prohibiting employees from attempting this shortcut.

Light It Up

Here's a more fun suggestion. Why *just* post a sign or share a calendar? Why not go fully modern and install a remote-controlled light outside your door—one that you turn on when you're on a call or in a meeting (like those old recording booths). This is also a fantastic tool for young children; they may not be able to read, but they know that when the light is on mommy, daddy, or Uncle Ben is on a call and can't look at the cool Lego kit they just built. (Not that we know from experience.) This might be a stretch to turn into a policy for those you manage, but no matter what style of notification and protection you take or recommend, it's important that everyone knows to do more than just shut their door.

Maintaining a Culture of Homestead Humanity

Working remotely often means working from home. And that home includes a variety of things that can be seen and heard on a phone or camera. Everything from a plant to a piece of art to your walls are just as much on camera as you are. Add in the occasional family member, friend, or pet who walks on screen or makes a noise in the office, and you've opened yourself up to a world of questions or feedback from co-workers:

"Oh is that a new plant?"
"I love that wall color!"
"Can we see the new puppy?"
"Did your son just . . . burp?"

Some of this is no different from the proximity world, where a fun mug, photos of family, and personal choices of art are on display. But what often separates the proximity from virtual working world is that instead of commenting on a static photo of your dog, your co-workers have a chance to see Scruffy on-screen every day—they can see him age, play, eat . . . lick himself. You get the idea.

Let's look at a few guidelines for homesteading your home office.

Be Mindful of What's On Display

Depending on where you take your calls or video conferences, anything you own could be on display and it doesn't hurt to take stock of what people will see on screen. This reflects what you don't want them to see just as much as what you *do* want them to see.

In the same what that you would consider your cubical background while doing a Facebook Live video, it doesn't hurt to take a curated approach your environment. Do you want to use the space to express yourself through your personal art, smart lighting, or maybe a view into your gorgeous back-yard? Or, would you rather hide your surroundings? You may not want your co-workers to seen those piles of unread mail, your messy kitchen, a dying plant, or that clothing-covered treadmill.

Maintaining the corner of your world that co-workers or clients can see is just as important in the virtual workplace as in the proximity-based one. Maybe even more.

Make Space for Insight Into Virtual Life

Some work environments are casual, whether virtual or proximity-based. In these cases, people will frequently ask how your spouse, children, or pets are. In the virtual environment, people might call out to your spouse or child on a call or video conversation, knowing they are within ear's reach, and expect to hear some kind of reply. Or maybe they'll ask to see the new baby or what the kids are wearing for Halloween. They will ask where you got the wallpaper in the background or if you're loving the new coffee maker they can see behind your shoulder.

Where this is the norm, allow it to be the norm. Create space for these conversations in the first or last few minutes of a call. Invite people "into" each other's space where it applies. Recreating a kind of "show and tell" atmosphere to talk about what kind of coffee you're drinking, the music you're listening to, or the new art you have on the walls is a fantastic way to build morale, familiarity, and team building. Just make sure everyone is on board.

When Transparency's Not Welcome, Build a Policy

While it's normal to occasionally notice and mention something you can see or hear in the background of a co-worker's home or office, culturally this isn't always welcome and needs to be curtailed. In these cases, it's important to develop some sort of guidance or policy explaining that you encourage employees at Company XYZ to refrain from commenting or expressing interest in another co-worker's or client's virtual surroundings. Remember—the proper way of discouraging something is to do so in writing.

A Few More Thoughts

✓ **Remember a quiet, uninterrupted virtual workplace is not inhuman.** Working remotely or from home can lead to a number of potential interruptions, but that doesn't mean they're all invited or welcome to a productive workday.

✓ **Keep the noise down.** You might need a written policy requesting people conduct their work away from noisy, interruptive, or distracting environments—even if those noises, interruptions, or distractions come from loved ones or pets. When those policies are repeatedly broken, they can be addressed appropriately as policies and not as personal attacks.

✓ **Don't mistake what you see with what you should say.** Just because you can see something in the background doesn't mean it needs to be addressed or discussed. Just as someone's new haircut doesn't always need mention, the same goes for a new background, piece of art, or family member.

Signing Off

In a proximity-based or virtual scenario, life goes on around us when we're working. Working virtually, especially when that means working from home, has many advantages, such as being able to spend more time with the ones you love. They are important to you and bring joy to your life. But it's also essential to remember that work is important too, and it should continue as seamlessly and uninterrupted as possible, no matter where you're working from. Being proactive in managing your environment and the environment of your employees will go a long way to successfully balancing work life and home life— no matter how many puppies, kitties, or children you have or co-workers want to see.

28.

Office Romance

One plus one equals two, even in the virtual workplace. But did you also know that more than a third of those "twos" are fired once their office romance is exposed? Another 17 percent resulted in a transfer and yet another 5 percent resulted in some form of lawsuit (Challenger, Gray, and Christmas 2018).

As a manager you can't be caught thinking, "But online relationships are just that—online—who's going to know?" Is company equipment being used to fan the flames of a relationship? Are they texting on a company phone? On company time? Is there a swell of instant messaging or are logs of emails filled with adorable love messages building up on an organizational platform?

This happens far more than you realize. In 2017, the wedding website The Knot surveyed more than 14,000 engaged or recently married individuals and reported that 19 percent of brides met their spouses online (Ross 2017). Fun fact, did you know that 100 percent of virtual employees also work online? Because that's the same "online." Another fun fact? In the stationary workplace, more than 38 percent of people have dated someone in their office at least once and more than 31 percent said that romance led them to the altar (Careerbuilder 2011).

So take the fact that online relationships have become ubiquitous and mix it with the prevalence of romance found in the office, and the likelihood is quite high that, as a virtual manager, this is something you will eventually have to deal with. The question you should be asking yourself is simple: How should I or my organization handle this dynamic?

Do you know your company's office romance policies? Do they contain elements that pertain to online and virtual environments? If you're reading this chapter, we would suggest they should. Let's talk about a few areas to consider.

Make It Clear: No Means No

Statistics are just that and sometimes you don't want to become one or have an employee of yours become one. As a manager, the easiest thing to do is to create and enforce a policy that sets the expectations of professional conduct and any consequences of office romance.

While workplace romance can feel like a taboo topic, you still need to address it. The potential for online romance is real in the virtual workplace, because it's surprisingly easy for employees build virtual relationships and think they're in love with co-workers they've never met. After all, we've spent the last 28 chapters stressing how easy it can be to build real relationships online as a manager.

As you can probably tell by now, we're fans of being straight-shooters. So, when it comes to office romance the key is being fully transparent and simple with your policies about it not being OK. Keep your policy short and unsalacious, like this one:

At Company X we do not allow or condone office romance of any kind, either in-person or online. Please refer to your employee handbook for further details and any disciplinary actions that will be taken for those engaging in an office romance, up to and including termination. If you have any additional questions or concerns, please talk to your manager or human resources.

Make It Possible: Create a Relationship Contract

Maybe it's not a good fit with your organization's personality to fully prohibit office romance. Instead, a better fit could be to build a few processes and policies that govern its existence in the workplace and online. This process would include a two-party system of disclosure—like a relationship contract submitted to a manager or HR. Relationship contracts not only protect the two people who are considering or engaged in a romance, they also help to protect the organization as an employer and you as a manager.

In addition to the general disclosure of the relationship, the contract should also address a few other things to ensure both parties fully understand your virtual workplace policies, such as:

- What virtual office equipment can and cannot be utilized within the nature of said relationship.
- How overt displays of affection are prohibited at work, including email, workplace technology, and conference calls.
- How employees must behave professionally and in a business-like manner while at work as well as at all company functions.
- That romantic squabbles should be left outside the workplace.

- The appropriate and inappropriate use of emojis; yes, emojis. Have you seen how painfully overused the heart or heart-eye-smiling emojis are in the early stages of love? What about some of the others? You know what we mean . . . the eggplant, the pointer finger, and the OK sign? They represent a misuse of company equipment if not addressed.

In addition to mutual disclosures, a solid relationship contract should also address several standard issues, no matter the virtual or proximity nature of employment. These issues might include:

- protection against harassment
- non-fraternization policies
- direct report and manager-based romantic situations.

All in all, the point of a relationship contract is to appropriately acknowledge the voluntary nature of the relationship. The disclosures should contain a reminder of the company's harassment, discrimination, and retaliation policies, as well as a clear acknowledgment that the relationship is consensual. And they should support any way the employees can find one another—online and off—therefore representing an understanding of how office technology use will and won't be tolerated within the relationship.

Make It Safe: Give People an Appropriate Voice

We are in a new era of workplace relationships and sexuality. And as such it's important to not only give people a voice to mutually declare a romance, but also to effectively decline office romances or report unwanted romantic advances.

In addition, companies and managers should not make the mistake of building policies and language that inherently gender or specify sexuality between two consenting parties. You might consider bringing in an outside consultant to help navigate LGBTQ topics and cultural understandings.

And we get it, all these considerations might make you far more prone to go back to the top of this chapter and re-read the "no means no" section. However, we implore you to consider wise, progressive policies that feel purposeful for your organization and employees. Working in a virtual world often lends itself to even more easily attained exposure—social media, email, texting, and so on—and that means your organization should be very thoughtful about how to ensure the security and safety of its employees and their livelihood as a business practice and policy concern.

A Few More Thoughts

If you're dealing with an office romance issue in real time and don't have a current policy, we can assume a few things:

- You've stumbled on a virtual romance and it's affecting company resources.
- You've been told about a virtual romance and other employees are talking, too.
- You've discovered a virtual romance and you're just generally confused about how to deal with or address it.

Based on these assumptions, we have a few suggestions to offer:

✓ **Contact HR for support.** No matter what you think you do or don't need by way of guidance or support, you need to contact HR to address the lack of policy and how best to get your needs supported.

✓ **Don't write policies and procedures with a single example in mind.** If one couple or relationship reveals a flaw in your policy design, don't immediately make a bunch of policy-driven changes. Like any other policy, you need to consult with experts in the given field and your HR team to conduct the appropriate level of policy design and support the policy's broader implications.

✓ **Consult other organizational policies.** Your problem might be supported by other existing policies, such as inappropriate use of tech, communications, and the like. These policies likely offer ways to address the issues outside the formal relationship, which will still allow business-as-usual behavior.

Signing Off

One thing we can say with confidence is that much of what an effective proximity-based office romance toolkit demands—policies, disclosures, examples of technology conduct, and so on—are also necessary in a virtual setting. The difference is that it's not always as obvious to spot the virtual romance, so making it culturally conversational and easy to access your organization's policies and purpose is more important than ever. Communicate expectations up front to minimize awkward conversations later. This often means ensuring it's part of your larger onboarding and orientation models, and that romance doesn't come off as a taboo subject overall.

In the end, you want to be transparent and clear with your employees. They deserve at least that much when faced with trying to navigate the world of budding love and romance. That love stuff is hard enough without work over-complicating or under-addressing the consequences.

29.

Harassment and Bullying

We live in a world that seems to become more angry and volatile every day—especially in the casual or socially based online world. One result has been an increase in bullying and harassment. We've all seen the commercials about the kid who is bullied at school because he doesn't look like everyone else. And we've heard the stories about the female subordinate who's being harassed by her male superior in the workplace, threatening to destroy her career unless she does what he wants.

No matter the age, no matter the means, and no matter the vehicle, harassment and bullying are never acceptable. Every human being has the right to live their life in a way that is free from any type of harassment. We hope that increased awareness around this topic will one day lessen, and even eradicate, the bullying and harassment in stationary and virtual workplaces.

Despite being a problem everywhere, these behaviors manifest differently in the virtual workplace, so that's our focus in this chapter.

Let's Level Set, Shall We?

The definitions of harassment and bullying include a range of actions, from persistently annoying to creating an unpleasant or hostile situation to treating someone in a cruel, insulting, or aggressive fashion to forcing or coercing someone to do something. This abuse can happen verbally or physically, online or in person. These definitions are absolutely loaded with meaning and description, and a lot of different behaviors and actions can and do fall into them.

Bullying and harassment are easily recognizable when they are played out at their worst. But on the sliding scale of bullying and harassment, are you able to identify where it begins? What do you do as a manager when the situation is not black or white, but gray? And what needs to happen differently when this is taking place in the virtual workplace? Well, we have a few specific thoughts on that topic.

I Manage a Virtual Team; I Don't Have to Worry About This

Spend a few seconds on social media and you will likely encounter bullying and harassment. People tweet and post mean, aggressive, insulting, and even slanderous things to and about other people every second of every day. Why is this happening? Behaving inappropriately is much easier when people are protected behind a computer screen and anonymous screenname. In fact, for some, as they sit alone at their home computer with no one else around, that screen can become a type of Fort Knox—emboldening them to freely speak their mind.

Think of it this way: When you are walking down a street with a lot of other people, your natural reaction if you accidentally bump shoulders with someone is typically going to be a quick apology before you continue on your way. You have no protection—you are out in the open. Of course, that's not *why* you apologize; you do it because it's the right thing to do. However, when someone cuts you off on the highway, it's much easier to lay on the horn and make all sorts of gestures. (Disclaimer: We are *not* condoning this behavior . . . just suggesting it happens.) Somehow being within the confines of a large, metal vehicle empowers you to act differently than if that "protection" wasn't there. When protected by that armor, the "right" thing to do suddenly doesn't matter so much—you know? What about *your* rights? You have been offended and that other person? Well, they had it coming.

All of this is just to say that, sometimes, online bullying and harassment occurs from a place that feels safe to the bully. Unfortunately, this means that it can be more difficult to detect in the online workplace. On the bright side—thanks to screenshots and cut and paste—bullying in the virtual space is often easier to prove than bold, in-person bullying and harassment.

As an ethical and effective manager it is crucial, both ethically and legally, for you to take every report of bullying and harassment seriously. If you don't, you could find yourself in a world of personal and professional trouble down the line. When a report of bullying or harassment is brought to your attention, you *must* do your due diligence to investigate and get to the bottom of the situation.

What Does Virtual Bullying and Harassment Look Like?

Bullying and harassment occur on a sliding scale. Sometimes, it's beyond obvious that it's happening. Other times, it can be very subtle and difficult to discern whether the situation truly fits either definition. But you've heard the old adage, "Better to be safe than sorry." This is a fantastic time to put that into practice.

What does this look like in a virtual environment? If we look back at our definitions, it can be someone constantly putting someone down while on a conference call, calling someone names, or insulting them in front of others. If there are witnesses, it is easier to detect and prove. But this monster can also rear its ugly head in much more subtle ways. Perhaps an employee is bribing another employee to do their work using employer-supplied cell phones, or making sexual remarks or innuendoes or sending inappropriate memes or pictures through the organization's chat platforms.

This is not an exhaustive list. Many other situations—both more and less subtle—can arise among your staff, and the single most important piece of advice we can give you is to take each and every report of bullying or harassment seriously.

Be an Observer

It's hard to see bullying or harassment yourself in the virtual workplace because it is happening between two or more people who are not within your line of sight. Unfortunately, there are also many stories of people who feel bullied or harassed but are too afraid to say something because of potential repercussions. Even worse, some may even start to question whether what they are experiencing is truly harassment at all.

As a manager, this is just another reason to get to know your people. Don't let the fact that you don't all work in the same building deter you from talking to your employees on a regular basis—learn who they are and what makes them tick. It's important for so many reasons, but especially for the topic at hand. Even if an employee experiences something that makes them uncomfortable, they may not bring it to your attention for any number of reasons. If this happens, we believe that your gut will sense that something's not right if you've taken the time to get to know the person.

This is another time that you'll benefit from using video instead of the phone when working with your employees. Video allows you to have a more sensitive finger on the pulse of their anxieties, issues, and demeanor. While these things can be heard and felt on phones or even through the printed word, they truly are more noticeable on the video screen, which will allow you to be more open and forward with your questions and concerns.

Don't get so wrapped up in your own tasks that you forget to observe the temperature, actions, and behavior of your team. This doesn't have to take a lot of time, and can bring great rewards in the long run. While you can't make someone talk about something they do not want to talk about, if you've built a good rapport, they will likely feel more comfortable opening up if they have something to share when you ask if everything is alright.

What might be an indication that something is going on? Watch for some of these behaviors—your staff member:

- suddenly doesn't speak up as much in meetings as they used to
- begins to call out sick much more frequently
- is generally not themselves

- exhibits decreased productivity or quality of work
- seems melancholy or distant
- is having trouble focusing
- suddenly does not want to work with another member of your team
- starts requesting a change in their work hours.

Again, it's not an exhaustive list, but want to get you thinking about how you can begin observing your staff and recognizing when things are not as they should be. When you show that you have interest in and care for your staff, it makes for a comfortable environment where staff are more willing to come to you to discuss even the most difficult situations.

A Few More Thoughts

✓ **Document what you see as you see it.** You absolutely must be able to attempt to prove the series of events and how they progressed, as well as any action steps you and an employee may have taken toward trying to resolve the situation. Document the conversations you have with both parties and keep these notes in a secure place. If you find yourself in the courtroom to testify on the situation it's crucial that you're prepared and everything is documented.

✓ **Pay attention to shades of gray.** When a situation seems to fall in a gray area, the best thing to do is defer to the person making the report. If that person feels uncomfortable or threatened in any way—it absolutely feels like bullying or harassment to them—it's your job to take it seriously.

✓ **Prepare your people.** Once an employee comes to you with a complaint of this nature, instruct them to save emails, take screenshots of chat conversations, write up the details of specific incidences while they're fresh, and so forth so you can add it to your documentation.

✓ **Waste no time addressing these types of situations.** It is always a serious situation when someone comes to you saying they feel bullied or harassed. At that moment, nothing is more important. Recognize that it took a lot of courage for them to come to you, and make sure you show just as much concern for the situation in return. Also understand that if left unchecked, these situations can quickly escalate to dangerous places—and nobody wants that.

Signing Off

You need to be so careful when it comes to this topic. While you want to make sure you are doing your due diligence and investigating every situation that is brought to your attention, you also don't want to swing too far in one direction. Accusing someone of being a bully or harassing someone is a very serious thing, and it's not to be taken lightly. This is a time that you should reach out to your HR or ombudsman teams for council.

If you notice bad behavior in a meeting—say, someone talks down to or insults another employee—talk to that person one-on-one, either by video conference (which is preferred) or by phone. Give them the opportunity to course correct. One offense does not a bully make. We are not saying that behavior is OK, but maybe that person was just having a bad day and their actions were totally out of character. Give the situation a chance to settle after you talk and see if it works itself out.

That said, we really must emphasize one last time how serious bullying and harassment issues truly are—and how it is your job as a manager to take each situation seriously. We have all heard the horrific stories of how bullying or harassment led to people doing terrible and irreversible things. So be observant. Ask questions when necessary. Be proactive. And when a member of your staff willingly comes to you to confide about something that they are experiencing, remember that, if not handled properly, it could quite possibly turn into a life-or-death situation.

30.

Dealing With Loss and Bereavement

Losing a loved one is never easy. But when you're a virtual employee in a virtual world, it can sometimes feel all the more isolating. When things like this happen, you want to make sure that your lack of proximity doesn't get in the way of your ability to acknowledge your employee's loss and offer condolences, virtually.

Let's Level Set, Shall We?

Everyone handles loss differently. Some people need to be around others who can occupy their mind so they think a little less about the pain. Others prefer to be alone and deal with their grief in their own way and at their own pace. Still others are somewhere in the middle—they want to be around people, or not, depending on the moment and people. Whichever way you deal with loss, one thing is for sure—we all want people to acknowledge our loss and validate our feelings of grief appropriately. That doesn't change in a virtual world. In fact, reaching out to a virtual team member who just lost a loved one could mean more to that employee than you ever could imagine, simply because you don't spend time with them every day. It shows that you are thinking about them and care about them.

"How Can I Be Sensitive but Not Intrusive?"

When one of your staff members loses someone they love, as their manager, you will likely be the first person in the workplace to get the news. It is a normal reaction to want to reach out and comfort them, but how on earth can you do that for a virtual team member? Whether that team member is across the state or around the world, you can and should show your comfort and concern.

Here are a few things you can do:

- **Be respectful, especially if you've never met the person in real life.** As their manager, ask the employee what their level of comfort is with you sharing the news with the rest of the team, what specific information they're comfortable with you sharing, and whether they do or don't want to be contacted virtually by co-workers. Then be sure to abide by their wishes. Some people might not want their team to know what's happening. Others might not mind people knowing, but don't want to chat over phone or go on video. Being able to tell your team the person's communication preferences can help everyone avoid wasting time or making things unintentionally awkward.

- **Don't have the initial conversation over email or chat.** If your team member told you the news via email or chat, immediately pick up the phone and call them, or ask if it's OK to contact them over video. Too much can go wrong or be misinterpreted in an email or over IM, and in a situation like this, you want to make sure that your employee can hear the compassion in your voice.

- **As a team, send flowers and a card to the grieving staff member.** Or, if the family requests donations in lieu of flowers to an organization the deceased was involved with, make a donation on behalf of your team or organization, in addition to sending a sympathy card to the employee.

- **Look up your bereavement time policy.** Remind your employee what the bereavement policy is so they know how much time they can take off.

- **If at all possible, attend the funeral services.** This will mean so much to your employee.

- **Give them time.** Your employee may need a little time to adjust back into work. Allow for that time and be sure to check in with them often. And, if they need a little extra help with their work, recruit another team member or members to help temporarily.

- **Host a team video chat.** After things have settled a little bit, perhaps have a group video conference so the team can offer their condolences face-to-face. But only do this if it seems appropriate.

When It's One of Your Own

Something that's not pleasant to think about—but happens—is what to do when one of your own virtual employees passes away. Since you likely do not know the family, make sure you exercise an extra level of respect and sensitivity when it comes to many of the same steps we just discussed concerning sharing information or details with fellow staff members.

In these situations, you as the manager often become the single point of entry for people to grieve, communicate, and vent. This is normal and important. But you also need to make sure you take time to grieve, communicate your feelings, and vent to people you trust.

Here are a few other issues to consider when the death is with one of your virtual employees:

- **Company hardware.** Communicate with the family how to return any workplace materials, but wait until the time is right. As painful as it is, and as cold and unfeeling as it may feel, in a virtual world it's necessary to address the safe return of organizational materials.

- **Company software and email.** Many virtual organizations can turn off or re-route employee technologies, accounts, and files with the push of a button. We usually talk about this in connection with someone leaving the organization, but this is also something that needs to be done when an employee passes away.

- **Job responsibilities.** As the manager, you need to determine who can carry the individual's roles and responsibilities during this time of grief and transition. It isn't always easy to do, considering how everyone might feel, but the work will still need to be done and it needs to be reassigned.

A Few More Thoughts

✓ **Budget for anything.** This is an area that often needs some budgetary considerations because a virtual workplace can be anywhere and things like sending flowers or shipping back a work computer takes money and planning.

✓ **Create a plan.** Not to add a sobering element, but this could be your funeral. And does your team or your boss know how they might handle this? Doubtful. So it's important—like developing any other policies—to create a SOP or plan so anyone dealing with something as difficult as a company death knows what to do, who to contact, and how to handle the details.

Signing Off

Death and bereavement are never easy subjects to talk or write about. But our best advice to you would be to be respectful and sensitive, and keep the level of confidence that the staff member or their family has asked of you. Find out what your employee needs; remember, in their time of grief they might not think to come to you for help. Offer compassion and empathy and let them know that you are there and will help however you can while they are going through this tough time. Basically, think about how you would like to be treated, and then plan ahead for the inevitability of life.

Acknowledgments

Ben

Writing a book about things that have almost never been written about in the land of fiction is almost harder than anything I've ever attempted in nonfiction. And yet more insightful and rewarding than I could have ever imagined.

I've had many of the problems addressed in this book, but no place to go to find the answers. So, my writing partner Kathy Wisniewski and I often talked on the phone or texted or IMed—for hours at a time—not only about the idea of this book, but about much of what went inside it too. The real, practical, tactical problems we were facing and trying to solve became something we worked on together to make our virtual management lives a little better.

I am eternally grateful to Kathy for trusting me, trusting us, and trusting the idea of co-writing this book, virtually. Pretty meta, right? Our friendship has not only grown but blossomed throughout this process and I can't wait for our next adventures together.

I am also widely and eternally grateful to my husband and best friend, Joe. With both of us working from home, he was not just a kind springboard for thoughts and ideas, but also there for every frustration, celebration, struggle, and success throughout the entire process of writing this book, offering a kind word, a stern look, or a gentle, "Baby, you got this. . . ." I could not have done this without him.

I want to thank the entire team of people that helped make this book possible. From the amazing Maria Ho who connected me with ATD many years ago, to the kind and generous Ryan Changcoco who invited the conversation about a book, to our remarkable and tolerant editors Jack Harlow and Melissa Jones, to all of the astonishing people who submitted content for this book, and everyone else who helped forge and push everything along.

I want to thank everyone I've worked with in a virtual capacity—over the years there have been thousands of you. I may not have met you in person, but you still played both a significant role in my professional life and in the experience of this book. It's sometimes daunting to effectively communicate with, support, and manage people you've never "met" and might never "meet" and build strong, effective relationships of purpose. My experience with you is this book. I will never be able to thank you all enough.

And finally, I want to thank my mom and my cats. My mom for being the true "forward" of the book of anything great I've ever accomplished. And my many, many cats who often walked across my laptop messing up my flow, but also reminding me to take a break to scratch their chins and remember that there is a wonderful world to experience beyond my desktop.

Kathy

It was a dark and stormy night in 2008. Ben and I had both hit roadblocks in our professional lives as far as being able to find resources to guide us in the world of virtual management. We were both managing many volunteers virtually for the first time and we'd spend hours on the phone asking each other questions that had no answers—only best guesses. There was nowhere to turn for information about the ins and outs of virtual employment or volunteerism. As we were figuring these things out on the fly, we realized that we should write them down for our own future reference—and for others, as well. And so the dream of compiling our findings into a valuable and constructive book was born.

This book did not happen right away. In fact, we picked it up and put it down many times over the next decade, but the ember of our dream of being published authors was alive and well. Our goal was not to be published for the sake of being able to say we were published authors—we wanted to pave the way for those who would come behind us. We wanted to be pioneers in this space so that our reach could go further and wider, and so those who would read our book would find a much easier path than we did.

It is so surreal to think that we've finally reached the end of this process. We've done the hard work, had the difficult conversations, figured out the tough stuff to get us to this point where we can share our thoughts and experiences with you. So, a huge thank you to all of you who decided to pick this book up for your own reasons and mine the golden nuggets out of it. Even though we will never have the privilege of meeting most of you, you inspired us to push forward, and without you this book would not exist. We are humbled.

To my writing partner and one of my closest friends, Ben Bisbee, thank you for always graciously tolerating me every time I brought up writing this book. One. More. Time. Thank you for always being ready and willing to lean in to the conversations, the questions, the scenarios, and the hours upon hours of figuring this stuff out—always without hesitation. Your determination and drive, positive attitude and wit never cease to amaze me. I could not have asked for a better partner to do this with, and I am a better person for having done this with you. I look forward to many more years of being pushed out of my comfort zone with you. You truly are the best. Thank you.

What many people don't know—even those who are close to me—is that during the year we spent writing this book, I was personally going through one of the toughest seasons of my entire life. It was only my faith, my family, and my friends that gave me the fortitude to lean in to the many wonderful things that were also happening in my life, including this book. Writing this book was exactly the escape I needed and the light in the midst of a very dark time for me. So my acknowledgments could not be complete without thanking God; my parents, Bob and Lynn Murdoch; my lil sis, Kristin Evans who always finds a way to make me laugh; and my closest friends and mentors, Jenn, Toni, Deby, Joyce, Lori, Katie, and Pamela, who were there for me every step of the way, encouraging me and always showering me with unimaginable amounts of love and support. Thank you for bearing my burden with me so that I could focus on the wonderful and beautiful things in my life like this book. I am forever indebted.

To ATD—what an honor and a privilege to be brought into your family of authors. We have both learned so much from this process and are so grateful for this opportunity. Thank you to

Ryan Changcoco, Jack Harlow, and Melissa Jones for the time you spent patiently de-greening us as authors and opening our eyes to this world. Thank you, as well, to the staff at ATD that we did not have the privilege of meeting, but who had a hand in making this book possible.

Finally, I would like to thank everyone with whom I've ever worked virtually. This book is really about you. It's about discovering and implementing ways to work with all of you in the most effective and efficient ways while together we strive to make this virtual world, and the real world, a better place. It's the work that you all do that inspires us each and every day and this book is our attempt to do right by all of you. For your inspiration, I am eternally grateful.

References

BBC News. 2017. "Cheeky Interruption for BBC Guest." BBC News, March 10. www.bbc.com/news/av/world-39232538/bbc-interview-with-robert-kelly-interrupted-by-children-live-on-air.

Careerbuilder. 2011. "Nearly One-Third of Workers Who Had Office Romances Married Their Co-Worker, Finds Annual CareerBuilder Valentine's Day Survey." Press Release, February. www.careerbuilder.com/share/aboutus/pressreleasesdetail.aspx?sd=2%2F9%2F2012&id=pr678&ed=12%2F31%2F2012.

Challenger, Gray, and Christmas. 2018. "SURVEY: The State of Office Romances Post #MeToo." Press Release, Challenger, Gray & Christmas, February. www.challengergray.com/press/press-releases/survey-state-office-romances-post-metoo.

Discovery Education. www.discoveryeducation.com.

Global Workplace Analytics. 2018. "Telecommuting Trend Data." GlobalWorkplaceAnalytics.com, July. https://globalworkplaceanalytics.com/telecommuting-statistics.

Katz, E. 2017. "Remote Workforce NPS: The Most Important Metric You're Missing." Business 2 Community, March 2. www.business2community.com/business-innovation/remote-workforce-nps-important-metric-youre-missing-01785305#oWRIA4bsxOwz6011.97.

Missing Maps Project. "How We Work." www.missingmaps.org.

Occupational Safety and Health Administration. 2016. "Restrooms and Sanitation Requirements." U.S. Department of Labor, January 24. www.osha.gov/SLTC/restrooms_sanitation.

Rivers, A. 2016. "How Many People Check Their Smartphone in the Bathroom?" The Marketing Scope, April 7. www.themarketingscope.com/how-many-people-check-their-smartphone-in-the-bathroom.

Ross, S. 2017. "This Is Officially the Most Popular Way People Are Meeting Their Spouse." The Knot, November 15. www.theknot.com/content/online-dating-most-popular-way-to-meet-spouse.

Shemla, M. 2018. "Why Workplace Diversity Is So Important, and Why It's So Hard To Achieve." *Forbes*, RSM Discovery, August 22. www.forbes.com/sites/rsmdiscovery/2018/08/22/why-workplace-diversity-is-so-important-and-why-its-so-hard-to-achieve/#7013a9733096.

Wellin, J. 2017. "The Science Behind Why Your Gestures Look So Awkward on Video." Wistia for Marketing, September 6. https://wistia.com/learn/production/science-behind-gestures-on-camera.

About the Authors

Ben Bisbee is a dreamer, a doer, a madman with focus; the good kind of dangerous. A multi-sector professional with more than 20 years of experience building successful, award-winning community and development programs for organizations of all shapes and sizes, he is a nationally recognized author, speaker and problem-solver. As the chief vision officer at Rhinocorn, a design house for nonprofit innovation and advancement projects, Ben works to drive the focus and direction of the company's vision and purpose.

Considering himself a social technologist, Ben is quickly becoming known for his work in virtual technology and methodologies, helping to build strengthened relationships between humans and the technology they use to work, play, and engage. Ben lives in northeast Ohio with his husband, Joe, and their 10 cats.

Kathy Wisniewski, CVA, is a nonprofit professional who has been in the sector for nearly 20 years. Currently serving as the executive board administrator for the Histiocyte Society based in Pitman, New Jersey, she specializes in volunteer and board administration. She has a particular love for the international community as she scouts, plans, and executes the society's annual meeting in various locations around the world.

Kathy is also a Certified Health Coach and owner of True and Lasting Wellness. After so many years in the nonprofit sector and seeing firsthand how professionals are in danger of burnout and in need of more balance in their lives, she chose to focus her business on primarily virtual health coaching for nonprofit professionals, helping them discover and reach their health and wellness goals.

Both of these endeavors have honed Kathy's virtual management skills and given her a deep appreciation for the advantages of technology in being able to reach a larger audience in our virtual world. Kathy was born and raised in New Jersey and although she now calls northeast Ohio home, she will always consider herself a Jersey girl.

Index